PLEASE RISE!

PLEASE RISE!

Delinquent and Dependent Children,
a Community Responsibility

by Mozelle Hilliard

mott media
BOX 236, MILFORD, MN 48042

Scripture quotations are from the King James Version.

Copyright © 1977 by Mozelle Hilliard

All rights reserved

No part of this book may be reproduced or transmitted in any form or by any means, electronic or mechanical, including photo copying, recording, storage in any information retrieval system, or other, without written permission of the publisher. Brief quotations embodied in critical articles or reviews are permitted.

Printed in the United States of America

Library of Congress Cataloging in Publication Data

Hilliard, Mozelle, 1918-
   Please rise!

   Bibliography: p.
   1. Juvenile delinquency — United States — Case studies. 2. Juvenile courts — United States. 3. Juvenile corrections — United States. I. Title.
HV9104.H5   364.36'0973   77-6450
ISBN O-915134-19-5 pbk.

To

My husband, Ken,
and to our children,
Melodie and Sheri,
for the joy they have given me
as a wife and mother

Contents

Preface	11
Introduction	13
Part One: The Delinquent Child	**15**
1. "God don't really love me" — JODI	17
2. "Look how smart I am" — MIKE	33
3. "Was love enough? — DANNY	49
4. "It takes more than a biological act" — DON	61
5. "Without Me, you can do nothing" — LENNY	71
Part Two: The Dependent Child	**85**
6. "The Lord is not through with me yet" — WENDI	87
7. "An angel for a mother" — LIZ	99
8. "A home is more than rooms separated by walls" — BART	111
9. "I looked in the mirror" — SUZANNE	123
10. "No use for child beaters" — GINGER	133
Part Three: View of the Problem and Solutions	**149**
11. Scope of the Problem	151
12. Causes and Responsibilities	163
13. The Christian Answer; the Christian's Responsibility	169
Appendices	177
1. Historical Background of the Juvenile Justice System	179
2. Structure of the Juvenile Court	181
3. Process Used in the Correction of Juveniles	187
4. Laws Significantly Changing the Juvenile Correctional Process	191
Glossary	193
Suggested Readings	199

Foreword

I feel that Mozelle Hilliard's book, *Please Rise*, should be read by anyone who has interest in the juvenile court. For that matter, this book is of great value and contains useful information for educators, parents, and everyone interested in children and the problems they face.

We have been very fortunate to have had the services of Moe Hilliard to assist us in the Pierce County Juvenile Court over this past decade. She has served as the liaison officer between the court and the Tacoma Public Schools. In this capacity, she has supplied the court with useful and essential information about a child's school performance for the use of the court in determining a proper disposition in juvenile proceedings. Likewise, she has provided the schools with useful information concerning children appearing before the court. She has enjoyed an excellent reputation and has good working relationships with all persons, both at the schools and at the court.

It is hoped that all persons reading Mrs. Hilliard's book will become aware that the responsibility for our children having problems requiring court attention is not only with the school, the parent, or the court. Often the problem arises from the *public* attitude or opinion, causing, for example, family breakdowns or school discipline problems. The community has a responsibility in seeing that the family relationship is preserved and protected, and in preserving proper atmospheres for the raising of children.

Donald H. Thompson
Juvenile Court Judge
The Superior Court
State of Washington

Preface

Welcome to my world!

National concern over juvenile delinquency has increased greatly. Equally as significant has been the growing national effort to provide for the dependent child. The juvenile courts across the nation are judicially responsible for the rehabilitation and protection of delinquent and dependent children.

Please Rise is written to acquaint the reader with the scope of the problem and its significance. Statistical data, information about the historical background, the structure of the court and of the juvenile correctional process are given to stimulate further thought and research. The case studies are presented in realistic dialogue and description in order to give an emotional and spiritual challenge to action and involvement. The case studies described have not all reached satisfactory solutions. The only real answer, the only abiding solution is found in God's plan. Only as individuals, as part of the body of Christ, become involved, will the most significant purpose for *Please Rise* be attained — to give glory to God and to be used as a service in His kingdom!

Please Rise is an outgrowth of thirteen years experience in working with court-connected youth, their parents or guardians and their probation officers and staff from community agencies. Personally, I have had to come face to face with the need to be of spiritual service. Professionally, I have had an opportunity for service in working with thousands of young people and their families at various levels of involvement. In my work as Juvenile Liaison Officer, my primary function relates to the educational opportunities provided for each child. In presenting an effective, workable plan in any given situation, it is very often necessary to involve persons other than those in the educational process. The position has required sensitivity and understanding on one hand, and knowledge of community resources on the other hand.

Materials used in this book have come from personal experiences and observations, interviews conducted with young people and their parents presently or previously connected with the court, and interviews with Pierce County Juvenile Court staff, the Youth Guidance law enforcement staff, community agencies and school district staff. Research materials were obtained from the local FBI office, the local newspaper, the Pierce County Juvenile Court, and selected readings.

In all of this I have sensed that those involved have resigned themselves to the improbability of ever reaching a viable solution to the problem. Because of my personal conviction that there is a solution, *Please Rise* became a reality, brought to life with spiritual values and opportunities ever in view, and born in the midst of life where these children struggle and work and hope for a brighter tomorrow!

Special acknowledgment is made to Mr. Harold Mulholland, Director of Pierce County Juvenile Court Services who spent many hours editing and advising in the writing of *Please Rise*; to the court-connected youth interviewed and to the parents and probation officers of these young people for their willingness to share a portion of their life with the hope of helping others. Without them this could not have been written.

My deep appreciation is expressed to Mr. E. A. Patchen, Executive Secretary of the National Educators' Fellowship for his encouragement through the years to share these experiences through the written word and for his faith in believing *Please Rise* can be used for the Glory of God.

To my family, thank you for allowing me the time to be a part of the lives of these young people and for your love and encouragement through the years and for your confidence in believing that this work is of Him! Without the sacrifice of each member there would have been no possibility *Please Rise* could have been written.

Introduction

"Please Rise!"

How often, over the past twelve years, I have heard those words spoken by the clerk as she preceded the juvenile court judge into the court room. Frightened, tense youth turn tear-filled eyes to the door of the judge's chambers and rise with heavy heart, knowing that judgment has begun. Parents, tears streaming down their cheeks, stand, shocked and grief stricken, as the petition is read charging their beautiful daughter or handsome son with a delinquent act, a violation of the law.

How often as I have sat on the court room chairs I have heard the stories of broken homes, rejected children, unloved and unloving parents, abused and abandoned infants, and have witnessed family members turning on one another, lashing out, spewing obscenities in every direction, making accusations and placing blame. How frequently I have listened to excuses made by parent and child as to why the law was broken, only to hear the judge remind the speaker "that may be an explanation, but it is no excuse."

How often I have heard the gasps, even moans, as the judge, acting within the framework of the law, brings judgment! He reminds parent and child of the past opportunities that have been given for correction of the problem and then declares "the last chance has been given — you must now be responsible for your actions."

That is the tragic part of the experience.

But how often during the past years I have had the privilege of sitting with a broken-hearted boy or girl, one who has broken the law, and has been locked in a cell for a period of time, and have been able to help him understand his responsibilities and his need for change in attitude and interaction with others. It has been my privilege to talk with parents, listening to the explanation of all the effort and time invested in the life of the child who is now in legal difficulty — soon to face the judge, charged with committing a serious violation of the law. What a thrill it is to see the light of understanding appear on a face, an expression of hope, an added strength to move forward with confidence in being able to do a better job, when a word of encouragement, a helpful suggestion, is given to them.

Frequently I am asked the question, "How can you stand to be in this kind of work? Isn't it depressing?" My answer is always an emphatic "NO!" I am in my position by divine appointment, and no service is depressing when one goes in His strength. I believe in young people. To me they are fascinating. There is no greater resource in all the world than a young person — especially one who comes to know the Lord, is totally committed to Him, and takes his place in God's service. I believe the majority of parents love their children and want the very best for them. I believe they work very hard at it. But the parent who seeks the Lord's guidance has that added Dimension that makes the difference in child rearing. Depressed? NO! The word is EXCITED!

This year thousands of young people throughout the nation, between the ages of eight and eighteen, will face a juvenile court judge, alleged to be delinquent, which means the child has committed an act that is in violation of the law and that, except for the child's age, would be considered a crime, or felony. If the facts are proven, he will be adjudicated a delinquent by the court.

More thousands of children will come to the attention of the juvenile court this year as dependents. The dependent may include the incorrigible or the truant as well as the battered, abused, neglected, or abandoned child. Of the latter category, some have broken bones, some have been sexually abused, some are victims of incestual relationships, some have been burned by a cigarette touched to the tongue or a hand held under a hot running faucet. The small fragile bodies bear the marks of abuse!

Please Rise tells the story of just a few of the court-connected young people whom I have seen before the juvenile court judge during the past several years. These are factual cases. Permission has been granted in each case to tell the story. The names have been changed for obvious reasons. Conversation as recorded in the court hearing is not verbatim, but is indicative of the interaction and exchange between participants in such hearings.

As you read *Please Rise*, you may multiply each case many times over, for each week brings to the attention of the court many, many young people who are experiencing similar difficulty. True, each case has its own particulars, but the thread of spiritual need runs through all.

Part One

The Delinquent Child

Chapter 1

The delinquent child has become a major concern to social agencies and citizens of the nation — concern for wasted resources as well as rising dollar costs. The loss of human resource is appalling. Not all adjudicated delinquents are rehabilitated. Often a life is wasted. While observing and interviewing a child alleged to be delinquent, and waiting for his court hearing, one cannot help but think, "What wasted potential."

Much has been written about the causes of delinquent behavior. An equal number of pages have been devoted to suggesting solutions. The complexity of the problem arises in part from the fact that the behavior of the alleged delinquent is so various, so that the term itself — juvenile delinquency — is difficult to define.

What Is Juvenile Delinquency?

Delinquency is defined differently in various states. Generally speaking, the Juvenile Code defines a delinquent child as one who is under a specified age and who has violated the laws of the state, an ordinance of a town, city, or county, or any federal law, or law of another state defining a crime, and whose case has been referred to the juvenile court by any jurisdiction whatsoever. A delinquent act is one committed by a child under a specified age which, if he were beyond that age, would be considered criminal.

What Constitutes a Juvenile Act?

Among the acts for which young people are referred to the court are prostitution, rape, indecent exposure, child molesting, and sodomy. Armed robbery, burglary, breaking and entering, vandalism, larceny, and arson. Possession, use, and sale of drugs, use and possession of alcohol. Resisting arrest, auto theft, assault, homicide, and forgery. Glue sniffing, purse snatching, carrying a concealed weapon, possession of stolen property. There are many more categories.

Any criminal act an adult may commit, may also be committed by a juvenile. There are no limitations. Children are just as capable of violent crime as adults. In many instances they demonstrate more destructive intent.

How Are Juveniles Brought to Court?

The majority of referrals are made by law enforcement personnel — city police, sheriff's deputies, state patrol, Federal Bureau investigators (FBI), fire inspectors, security officers in stores and in schools, and immigration authorities. Referrals are made to officers by various agencies or individuals. For example, school administrators often find it necessary to call for police assistance. Citizens are also frequently involved in reporting incidents. In fact, it is the responsibility of anyone having knowledge of the possibility of a delinquent act being committed to report this to a law enforcement agency. It is then the duty of the investigating officer to decide whether the evidence is sufficient to warrant arrest and referral to the court.

In addition to law enforcement referrals, there are instances when a parent reports the delinquent act of a child. A parent may find quantities of marijuana or other controlled substances in the child's room. Or, it may be that a parent finds in the home articles which do not belong to the family. If his inquiry reveals that his child is in possession of stolen articles, he must report it — if he is honest, and if he cares enough for his child. Parent referrals are made for other reasons, such as theft of money from the home, taking the family automobile without permission, or incorrigibility.

Many parents believe children should be taught to obey the law. By being obedient to the law themselves and not tolerating the child's violation, they provide an effective example. A child sees respect for the law in action. He learns to be accountable for his actions. He hopefully learns obedience to his parents. Obviously, the law abiding parent takes a risk when he takes this stand. The child may turn against him, he may choose to live elsewhere, or he may become more deeply involved in delinquent acts in his hurt, confused feelings. The Christian parent who finds himself in this position has the assurance that God will undertake in establishing familial relationships. He understands that he is accountable to God for his family, that he must provide guidelines to live by, and that he must set the example.

Difficult though it may be to make such a referral, the violation must be worked through. This may require a remand to the court. In such a case, the parent has the opportunity to stand beside the child, not condoning, but being supportive. No action the court may take will have such an impact or be so effective. The unaccepting child's attitudes can be changed as the parent continues to work with him, perhaps receiving supportive services from the court or a community agency. It will take time. But the family structure provides the security of limits, laws, and consequences if these are violated.

Probation officers are also a referral source to the court. A child on a reporting basis to a probation officer may reveal further acts of delinquency in conference sessions with which the officer must deal. He may file a petition for a court hearing, so that judgment will be made by the juvenile court judge. Or he may choose the option of lock-up for a designated period of time. The probation officer's priority is the welfare of the child. He decides what action he feels is best to take. But he must take action. He too is responsible before the law.

A young person may refer himself for the commitment of delinquent acts. When the pressure becomes too great, he may choose to turn himself in. This is commendable. It does not, however, make him any less responsible. He must be held accountable for his actions.

What Are Delinquents Like?

They are just like the young person you may have in your home. Just like your son or daughter. Just like the girl or boy next door! Some of them are beautiful, talented, and brilliant. Others are careless in dress, academically unmotivated, habitually truant, antagonistic to the system. Some are ambitious and energetic, setting goals and striving to reach them. Others live for the day, taking each day as it comes, taking everything offered and asking for more. Some youngsters who appear in court respect authority, get along well in school with staff, and have no difficulties with parental authority. Others insist on their own rights.

No family is immune. Children who appear in the court are from all walks of life — sons and daughters of pastors, and lawyers, school staff members, law enforcement personnel, even judges. They come from every kind of home imaginable — poor homes, middle class, wealthy. They represent the pampered and the deprived. Some have had everything. Some have had nothing.

To truly characterize the juvenile delinquent is impossible. Contrary to what is often believed, these children are not anti-social. They participate in sponsored social activities along with non-delinquent youth. They take part in sports and school activities, and often belong to informal groups as well. They include school drop-outs and high achievers. More often older youth are involved than younger ones, but the age level is dropping. They may be of any race.

Many of these children have organizational ability. They use this skill in planning the delinquent act. Their immaturity keeps them from realizing that there has never been a "perfect crime" committed. The feeling that he will not be apprehended excites a certain type of young person to become more bold. When in court, he frankly admits his motive — to see if he could get away with it! On the other side, the court often sees the child who knows he will be apprehended, yet continues. He explains it by saying he wanted to do what he was doing, or that he was just going along with his friends. Very often he adds, "Whatever I get, I deserve!" To some it is a game. To others it becomes a way of life.

Attitudes exhibited in court both by the juvenile and the parents are very revealing. They present many varied faces.

For example, the sexually delinquent girl before the court usually appears more physically mature for her age than is expected. She displays a pseudo-confident manner, giving the impression of a little girl playing house. Her attitude toward her male partner may vacillate from "he loves me" to "that rotten bum ... I hate him!" She may act impatient with the court, intimating she is knowledgeable about preventative measures. Or she may have a "whither thou goest I will go" attitude toward her newfound "love," expressing a desire to bear his child. She may act deeply shocked at the suggestion she is loose, declaring he is the only one. Or she may frankly admit she enjoys variety.

The parents of the girl may reflect any variety of attitudes, from shock to disbelief to anger to lack of concern. In some cases, it appears especially difficult for the father to be supportive. He may be very angry, though this may not be directed toward the child. He may appear gravely concerned. Mothers often weep. They tend to be more verbal. Blame is cast on the "wrong friends." At times parents adopt an attitude of resignation. The child they once knew is replaced by a woman, or at least a body that is indulging in womanly acts! An observer senses the breach: it will never be the same between them. As unbelievable as it seems, there have been parents who are elated: "I always wanted to be a grandmother, now I will" was the way one mother expressed her feelings about her fourteen year old daughter's pregnancy. And then there are parents who are unconcerned, presenting a cold, passive "out of my hands" attitude.

Come meet Jodi, a teenage prostitute. Here is her story.

JODI ...

"God don't really love me."

Jodi's nonchalant attitude and manner — her composure and unconcern — as she moved through the door leading into the court room permeated the room as she walked to her designated seat. She turned to her probation officer and suggested, "This looks good ... shall I sit here?"

"Yes," replied Mrs. Fremont. "When the judge enters, Jodi, be sure to stand. You will have your opportunity to speak with him and I want you to sit up, act like a young lady, and answer him with respect."

"I am a young lady. Geez, you guys! I haven't done anything! He should respect me too! Will he?" Jodi lashed back.

The guardian ad litem, appointed to represent Jodi in court, moved restlessly in his chair. This attorney was employed by the court to protect Jodi's constitutional rights, and to act as her guardian and make a recommendation to the court as to what disposition he felt would be in her best interests.

"Jodi, listen to me," began the attorney. "You are in serious trouble! What more do I have to tell you? I am really upset over your attitude. You act as though this is a summer picnic and everyone is obligated to bring the goodies and your only role is to enjoy them. Now, snap out of it, or I don't know what could happen to you. Are you listening to me?"

"Yeah," Jodi's voice had an angry tone to it. "I hear you ... now leave me alone!"

The probation officer and the attorney exchanged glances. Mr. Newell walked over to Mrs. Fremont.

"I don't know, I just don't know," he said. "This is a real problem! He is going to throw the book at her if she doesn't cool it!"

"I know," answered Mrs. Fremont, "but we have done our best. Maybe that is what she needs."

Mr. Newell turned and went to the parents, who were seated directly behind Jodi in the court room. Mr. and Mrs. Phillips appeared to be in their fifties. Mr. Phillips seemed tired, the strain of the past few weeks evident in his expression. Small in stature, he was neatly attired, though not stylishly so. Mrs. Phillips was a large woman. She was dressed neatly, wore a hair style which was somewhat contemporary but with a hint of the style of the sixties, and applied make-up tastefully. She did not appear as weary as her husband who was holding down two jobs to support the family and had had very little rest before coming to court. She also seemed less concerned than her husband over the current situation.

A conversation with Mrs. Fremont revealed that Mrs. Phillips was better able emotionally to enter into a discussion regarding her daughter than was Mr. Phillips. In fact, the mother was almost casual in her conversation about the events of the past few months. This casual approach was confirmed by the guardian ad litem as he said, "I will do what I can, but you know she does need some help. Please try to relax, and when the judge asks your opinion, don't hesitate. Be very frank with him."

"I am relaxed," replied Mrs. Phillips. "I will tell him what he wants to know."

Mr. Phillips' sigh was audible. He shifted nervously in his chair, folded his hands, and then began to work them together. The guardian took his seat, shook his head, and began to look over his notes.

Mrs. Fremont attempted once again to reach Jodi. "This is a court, Jodi. Be careful, please."

Jodi turned to face her probation officer. "I know what I am doing . . . I aint doing nuthin', so what is all the fuss about? Do you want me to stand on my head . . . what do you want?"

"No, Jodi, turn around. Be quiet."

"Geez!" Jodi's tone was defiant. She turned around, slumped down in her chair. Her next comments were not audible.

The court record indicated Jodi's problems started the summer before. She had begun going to the Mall, a hang-out for young people using drugs and involved in unlawful activities. It was also the gathering place for young people whose parents prohibited their associating with certain "friends." Jodi was not a popular girl at school. She was not particularly attractive, her complexion was bad, she was not well groomed. When she was introduced to some black boys by one of the girls she had made friends with, she readily involved herself with a group with whom she felt accepted, and even appreciated. Her immaturity prevented her from evaluating the reasons underlying the attention of the young black fellows. One thing led to another. Jodi became sexually involved with not one, but several black youths, young men around twenty years of age.

While on one of her evenings out with her girl friend, she entered a downtown tavern and pin-ball establishment. There she met Ralph. She became his girl. From her first meeting with him, she went to bed with him. Ralph was from a city nearby. In order to be with him, Jodi ran from home. She joined him in a hotel room. He put her on the street to prostitute to earn their keep. Jodi returned home within a few weeks, but shortly thereafter left again, this time with her girl friend. They joined Ralph, and once again Jodi was on the street, prostituting. So was her girl friend, who was soon arrested and directed the police to Jodi. Her parents brought her home and her father entered her in the juvenile detention facility.

I had called before visiting the home to ask permission for the interview. Mrs. Phillips readily agreed. After a calm, casual conversation with her, I left feeling Jodi's needs were tremendous. Mrs. Phillips indicated Jodi spent a great deal of her time in her room, "listening to her records, or radio ... never had too many friends until she met this Cathy. It was all because of this no good Cathy that Jodi did the things she did. Cathy introduced her to the blacks ... she never would have run away if she had not been with Cathy. I knew she was going to bed with the blacks. I even asked her about it, but she never did tell me until this last time. We had her examined for disease, and were going to have her tested to see if she was pregnant, but she isn't, so we don't have to go through that. Her dad works hard. When she run away the first time, she was gone until after Christmas. I didn't know what to do with her clothes I had bought, so I took them back to the store. When she came home, her dad felt sorry for her and bought her a radio. But she didn't stay home long. One day she got a phone call and I knew it was that Ralph. I don't know how she done it, but somehow she let her clothes out of the window and took them all to school with her the next day. The school called me to tell me she wasn't there, and I went to her room. Everything was gone ... I knew she went to Ralph.

"The first time she left," the mother continued, "she came home on her own. She didn't say what all went on, but I kind of suspected the worst. She seemed real happy, took her radio, and said she wasn't going to leave any more. In just a few days she was gone again. I know she is not using drugs, but she sleeps with every guy. She never did have a friend until she met this Cathy. Our other daughter gets real put out with her."

"Mrs. Phillips," I asked, "would you say you are a close family?

What kinds of things do you do together as a family? Are you able to communicate with one another? Do the girls discuss their feelings with you or their father?"

"No, they don't talk much. They are in their room most of the time. We don't do much. My husband works two jobs, tries to sleep a little and then goes back to work."

"Do you think I might be able to discuss this with your husband?" I asked Mrs. Phillips.

"You wouldn't be able to find him home. He works all the time," she replied.

"In that case," I said to Mrs. Phillips, "I will only be able to tell your part of the story. Tell me, what would you do, what kinds of changes would you make if you had the power to do so? What kinds of things could have been done differently in order to prevent this from happening?"

"Nothing," stated Mrs. Phillips, firmly. "I don't know of nothing. We do the best we can. The kids have a good home. It was that Cathy that caused this."

"Do you folks have a church home?" I asked the mother.

"No," she replied. "The neighbors took Jodi once or twice, but then she quit going. Said she didn't like it."

"Don't you feel it is important to attend church and have the girls involved in a church program? In that way, they would be able to meet young people with whom they could be accepted and could become part of a positive group."

"Oh, we don't have much time for that," was her answer. "We are not church people. We figure if we work and give the kids a living, that is enough."

I felt depressed when I left the home. Mrs. Phillips was courteous and polite, but the situation appeared so hopeless. The home itself was depressing. The blinds were pulled. The davenport and chairs were covered with pieces of material thrown over them. In order for me to be able to leave by the front door, a table in front of it had to be moved. As I walked away, I looked back. The unkempt yard could have been groomed and worked into a place of beauty. The closed-up house looked vacant. There was no sign of life around. Inside a mother — clean, comfortably dressed, seated among the covered furniture in a home with all the blinds pulled, watching the daily soap operas on television and saying "we are not church people ... it is all Cathy's fault ...." No expressions of love, no tears, no plans. Her tone of voice never changed as she casually acknowledged that she knew her daughter "was sleeping with them guys," that she "had her examined for disease" and she "didn't have to have her examined for pregnancy." "That Ralph just wanted her to make money for him ... the police can't do nothing about it ... he is not even of age ...."

Let's listen to Jodi tell her own story. For about two hours I sat conversing with her. She was crocheting a pot holder, seated in the chair with one leg under the other. She smiled frequently, at times laughed aloud, and on occasion showed anger at Cathy. She was neither nervous nor embarrassed.

"Jodi, tell me about yourself," I began. "What brought all of this about? How do you feel, where do you go from here?"

"You mean," Jodi smiled, "why did I run away, go to Ralph, and go out on the streets?"

"Yes."

"Well, it started last summer. I met these dudes, me and Cathy. Cathy is ... used to be my friend ... she ain't any more. They were nice to me. I thought I could keep them for a boy friend if I went to bed with them ... I did. I would meet some dude, go to bed with him, but then he wouldn't call. Then I met Ralph. I went to bed with him, and he called. I knew them other dudes was just using me ... but Ralph called. So, he bought some tickets for us and I went to him. That was before Christmas. I didn't think my folks would let me go out during vacation. When I was in school, I could skip school and meet him somewhere."

"Why did you 'sleep with guys,' as you put it, Jodi?" I asked.

"You mean the black dudes? Well, I don't sleep with white dudes ... they are mean to me. They tell me I am ugly, no good, and that nobody would like me. The black dudes call me 'lady', tell me I'm pretty, and make me know they enjoy making love to me. Besides, I didn't want to go back to school a virgin in September."

"What in the world do you mean by that?" I asked.

"Well, I wanted to show them I can get guys, too. Some of my friends liked the black dudes. They were doing it, so I did, too. That way, well, I am as good as they are." She looked at me and laughed. "Are you shocked ... most of the kids do it ...."

"No, Jodi, I am not shocked. That is not the word for it. I am wondering whether you know you are destroying yourself and others by your behavior," I answered her.

"Well, that is tough," she said, "I like it."

"Even for money?" I asked.

"When it is for money, it is for money. The other is for fun!" She smiled at me.

"Go ahead, Jodi. Finish the story," I requested.

"The first time I ran away," continued Jodi, "I met Ralph and he took me to a hotel room. He said if we were going to eat, I would have to go out on the street. I did. I made enough for us to live on. I stayed for about two weeks. Then I came home. My folks thought I was sleeping with Ralph, but they seemed glad to have me home. My dad bought me a radio, my mom had taken all of my Christmas clothes back to the store. I wasn't home too long and Ralph called on Saturday. On Monday I called him. On Tuesday I went to school. I said to Cathy I was going to go back to Ralph. I had ten dollars. She went with me. We got there about two o'clock. Around seven or eight, we went out. A police officer was following Cathy, so we went to the bus station and then went back to the hotel. Ralph was mad at us. We hadn't made any money. The three of us slept in the same bed. I was in the middle. He wouldn't touch me. The next day he asked me to leave for about forty-five minutes. He said he would make love to Cathy and then she wouldn't be so afraid of going out. I was mad! He slapped me around and said he was going to leave. I begged him not to. I promised I would get us some money. I went out, but I felt sick, so I came back. He was really mad then. He slapped me around some more. Then he said he was leaving. I talked to Cathy. She said she would leave. I begged him to stay. He promised he would. So we went out again. We didn't get any. We went out and came back three times, and Ralph was really mad. He really slapped me around then. I promised I would get us some money that night. We played cards until about seven. Then we went out on the streets. Cathy went by herself. Finally I got this old white dude. And I got some money."

"Jodi, how do you go about this — getting these men?" I asked.

"Oh, I just kind of stand there, walk around a little. Some old guy will come up. We start talking. I tell him I will do what he wants for say forty dollars. If he says he doesn't have that much, I say thirty-five. If he says thirty, I tell him okay for thirty minutes. He takes me to his hotel room, or wherever. Then I just tell him 'thirty minutes, that is it . . . then I am going.' If he fools around, that is his fault. I let him do whatever he wants to do for thirty minutes, then I go. If he just has twenty, and I really need the money I take that, but I always get paid first."

"How do you feel, Jodi, when this is going on? Doesn't this bother you? Are these dirty men, or bums, or what?" I asked.

"Oh, some of them are business men. They drive up in their car . . . some of them come down the street. They are looking for it. If they have the money and they are that stupid, I don't care. I don't think anything when I am doing it. I just let them do what they want to. Then I leave."

"But don't you think it is wrong to sell your body, Jodi?"

"Well, I have to have the money, so I do it."

"Why, Jodi, why don't you just stay home and live like other fourteen year olds? Why are you mixed up in this? Aren't you afraid you may be killed some day by some man?"

Jodi laughed. "No, I am not afraid. And why should I stay home? I like to do this."

"Well, anyway," Jodi continued, "I left the old man and went back on the street. I started walking where I thought Cathy would be. Some dude came along and said 'your friend got picked up by vice ... you better go hide or you will be picked up, too'. He described Cathy and I knew she was picked up. I went back to the hotel. I told Ralph. He said it was her own fault and she better not tell on us. Ralph told me to pay the hotel room and I thought he meant for me to pay for a week, so I gave the hotel all my money. Ralph was mad because we didn't have any food and he said he was hungry. We went to bed. The next morning he told me to go get some money. I got only fifteen dollars, but we had to have it. When I came back, we went out and ate. Then we were looking at furniture in a store. Ralph said he would get us an apartment. We played the pin-ball games for awhile and then we took the bus back to the hotel. The police came. Cathy had told them about us. I hate her. They took me to the Juvy Hall, and my parents came and got me. I was kind of mad at Ralph, too, 'cause I knew he kind of wanted Cathy. So I told them at the Juvy Hall I would sign against him. I did, but now I hear he is not of age and they can't do anything against him. I don't know what he thinks of me. I know he will beat me if he sees me again."

"How do you feel about him now, Jodi?"

"I still love him. He is a cool dude!" She smiled as she continued her crocheting. "But I don't ever want to see Cathy again. She snitched on us. I want her to get in trouble. She didn't have to come to the Hall." Jodi was angry now. She paused momentarily in her work. Her eyes flashed. "I could kill her!" she exclaimed. She began to crochet again.

"Jodi, tell me about your family. What kind of home life do you have? Your sister? What do you think of her?" I was hoping Jodi would be as candid in answering these questions as she had been about the other inquiries.

"You know, we are never together as a family. My dad is never home. I am not close to my parents, and I can't stand my sister. She is always screaming at me and arguing with me. My mom is always screaming and arguing with both of us. My mom won't let me go anywhere. That is why I would lie about where I was going. I don't think there is any love in our home ... I don't feel loved. And about my Christmas presents ... I told my mom I hated her for taking my things back ... my dad felt sorry for me and bought me the radio."

"Don't you feel you have hurt yourself and your parents, Jodi?" I inquired.

"I haven't hurt myself. Maybe I have hurt my parents. They haven't said."

"What do you plan to do with yourself?" I asked.

"I will just suffer through it all until I am eighteen. Then I am leaving. I don't like it at home. I don't like my family. But I know if I do get to go home, and run again, I will be caught. So maybe I won't run. I don't know. I still like Ralph and if he called me, I don't know. Maybe I would. I will see."

"Have you ever thought, Jodi, that you will have to account to the Lord for what you are doing?" I watched her intently as she sat silently for a moment, crocheting.

"Yeah, I have. I can imagine how terrible God must think I am."

"You mentioned wanting to be loved, Jodi. Do you know the Lord really loves you and wants you to come to Him with all these problems? Have you ever thought of perhaps giving Him a chance to really straighten things out? He can, you know."

Jodi, for the first time, put her crocheting down in her lap. She was determined in her next comment. "That bores me like hell! I am not for that church stuff. I fall asleep in church. I went with my neighbors once. They told me I was lost, needed to be saved! Boy, I stayed away from them. They kept coming back, but I had my mom tell them I wasn't going. So that is not for me!"

"Do you enjoy this life?"

"If you mean the old men," Jodi explained, "no. But I just let them do what they want to do and I got my money first. I don't think it is so bad, and it is the only way I have to make money. I don't think it is weird, or funny, or bad. I enjoy going to bed with dudes I like. But with the old guys, it is just for the money!"

"Jodi," I watched her closely as I spoke. "If you had a fourteen year old daughter, would you want her to act the way you do?"

Jodi hesitated for several seconds before she answered.

"No," she said, "but I won't ever have a kid. I am scared to get married. I couldn't stand the pain of having kids ... it would hurt ..." her voice trailed off.

Jodi shifted restlessly. I knew she wanted to end the conversation.

"Jodi, thank you for talking with me. I know it is late. You have crocheted quite a bit there, and it is pretty. So are you, Jodi."

Her head shot up. "You have got to be kidding. Nobody but dudes have ever told me that."

"But you are, and you have a lot to offer. You are smart, able to make good grades, and you could contribute a lot to your home and community if you really wanted to. But there is one thing for certain — with the ideas you have, I know one thing for sure."

"What is that?" she asked.

"Only the Lord can work this out for you, Jodi, and you know it.

And I know it. You better do some thinking. It is bigger than you are. You are in for big trouble and a totally ruined life if you continue. Back away while you can. Think about it. I will be around if you want to talk."

"I will," Jodi whispered, "I will."

And for the first time during the conversation, I felt Jodi was truly the frightened fourteen year old I had hoped to converse with, and not the bold, self-confident fourteen year old who was sure she had all the answers.

Seated in the court room, waiting for the judge to enter and observing Jodi, I was not so sure that she was ready to acknowledge the situation for what it really was. I was not sure she would make the effort needed to help herself, or to help others help her. I felt that the availability of the Lord to her was the farthest thing from her mind at the moment. She had that same smug smile, confident look, and determined expression on her face as she too sat waiting for the judge to enter. Her father sat, head bowed. Her mother looked straight ahead, expressionless. The probation officer appeared tense. The guardian ad litem continued to examine his notes.

"Please rise!"

The judge entered the room. "This court is now in session. You may be seated," stated the court clerk.

"This hearing comes on a petition filed by the parents, Mr. and Mrs. Phillips, alleging their daughter Jodi is an incorrigible girl in that she did on two occasions run away from the home, and on these runs did meet with her boy friend in Wallingford, where she was prostituting at his suggestion in order to provide funds to care for the two of them. The petition further alleges Jodi refuses to obey her parents, lies about her whereabouts, and is associating with male friends older than she, who are using her for illegal purposes. What is the position of your client, Mr. Newell?"

"Your Honor, the facts are not contested," replied the guardian.

"Very well. Mrs. Fremont, may I have the background information, please," stated the judge.

"Your Honor," began Mrs. Fremont, "I want to state I am concerned about Jodi. Her attitude leaves much to be desired, as Your Honor can observe."

"That I can," indicated the judge. "Sit up, young lady. You are in court!" His directive to Jodi was authoritative in tone. She sat up. "Now, look at me while Mrs. Fremont continues." Jodi looked at him, but she was obviously angry.

Mrs. Fremont went over the background. The information was

along the same lines as the investigation and Jodi's report had been.

"There is very little with which to work, Your Honor," concluded Mrs. Fremont. "I don't know why Jodi has the attitude she has. I don't know whether we have a girl here who is so psychologically damaged that she doesn't know right from wrong, or whether she has given up and just doesn't care. I am not sure she will ever make an appropriate adjustment in relation to herself without psychological or psychiatric help. I need to know more about what makes her do the things she does before I can make a recommendation. I do know that she cannot go home at this time. She has been tested and is free of venereal disease. She is not pregnant. But she is still emotionally attached to Ralph, and is not ready to cooperate with the court in rules of probation. I do not feel the parents are ready to have her home. I don't think they really understand what has been going on. I request of the court that Jodi be given a complete diagnostic work-up before disposition is made."

"Do the parents have anything to say?" asked the judge.

"We have given her a good home," the mother began, "and it is her friends. There is nothing wrong with her home." Mrs. Phillips looked at her husband. He sat, eyes on the floor.

"Mr. Phillips," the judge asked, "do you have any comments?"

"No, sir," replied Mr. Phillips.

"Don't you folks have any recommendation for me? This is your daughter. What should we do to help her?"

Mr. and Mrs. Phillips shook their heads. The judge scrutinized them intently for a moment or two, then directed himself to Jodi.

"Jodi, what about it? What is going on?" The judge looked demandingly at Jodi.

"Well, what do you mean? You have got the report. You tell me. You guys seem to know!" retorted Jodi. "There is nothin' wrong with me. You guys just make a fuss. Everything is okay."

"Let's get this straight, Jodi," said the judge. "You may think there is nothing wrong. But there is a great deal more wrong here than you think. You are a fourteen year old who is prostituting and you see nothing wrong with it. Your relationship to your parents is poor. You don't think school is necessary. You are going to bed with every fellow who asks you, in addition to prostituting! You tell me, do you really think there is nothing wrong?"

"Yeah, there is something wrong, I guess," Jodi lowered her head.

"Well, will you help us get it straightened out?" asked the judge. Jodi nodded her head affirmatively.

"Mr. Newell, what is your recommendation?" the judge directed the question to the guardian.

"Jodi tells me she wants to get out of here, but she does not want to go home. She admits she still likes her boy friend and she admits all that went on while she was on the run. I don't know that she would stay put if she were sent home. I really don't know what is best for Jodi, because so much depends on her and her parents. I will agree with Mrs. Fremont. A diagnostic evaluation is needed."

"Jodi, we are going to keep you here for awhile. I want to know more about your case. I want to know more about you. I want the worker here to get to know you and your parents better. We are going to run some tests to see if we can find out what the problems really are. After that, in about thirty days, we will come back in here and decide what to do. In the meantime, you stay here. I want you to know if you run, I will not have to be concerned about my disposition. You will have made it for me. I want you to cooperate. Do I have your promise?" The judge waited for Jodi to answer.

"I ain't gonna run," Jodi glared at the judge.

"Very well. We will see you again in about thirty days." The judge rose to leave the court room. All in attendance stood.

"Come with me, Jodi," said Mrs. Fremont. "Would you care to visit with your daughter?" she turned to Mr. and Mrs. Phillips. They shook their heads negatively.

"Wow! Big deal," said Jodi. "Geez," she said angrily as she left the court room with the probation officer.

During the next few weeks Jodi was to undergo several psychological tests to determine the depth of her emotional problems and to assist in the recommendation for disposition of her case, during which time she would remain in the detention facility. She would be living in the dependency wing, attending school and mingling with other children who were living at the Hall for one reason or another.

Jodi became one of the group. She was especially receptive to any attention directed her way. The most overwhelming aspect for her was really belonging to a group. Other girls sought her out. The boys were friendly with her. She was one of them. She did well in school. She seemed to enjoy herself, and always when she was observed she had a relaxed, easy manner and a pleasant smile.

Jodi and I talked several times. She was quieter and spoke more softly and more thoughtfully as time went by. She assured me the reason she lashed out about "God and them things" was that she felt so guilty, "and dirty, and awful."

When the dispositional hearing was held, following the psychological testing, Jodi went to live in a group home many miles away from her home town in order to break the ties of friends she had made. Living in a new environment, Jodi would have the opportunity to make a fresh start. She would have the chance to make new friends and to be a friend.

She would be able to examine her relationship with her parents, and they would have the same opportunity. She would receive encouragement and guidance from adults in establishing and achieving her goals.

I received a note from Jodi after she was gone for awhile.

"Thank you ... I still don't think I am pretty! Things are fine. I am studying hard. I have made a lot of girl friends. We do a lot of things, picnics, dinners, and play records. We watch TV and make pizza. I remember what you said. God don't really bore me ... it is just that I felt so bad about things. Maybe we can talk again when I get to visit home. I think I may get to soon. Love, Jodi."

Chapter 2

"A thief loses his freedom," the judge stated to a youngster involved in extensive theft of stereophonic equipment. "You must like music — especially if the equipment belongs to someone else. Why did you do it?"

"I guess I just ask for too much. There are eight kids in our family. I keep getting in trouble. My dad finally told me to go ahead but not to call on him if I got in any more trouble."

"Is that right?" the judge asked the father.

"Yes, it is," came the reply.

"Do you think that is right? Did you ever think of taking him to the woodshed? Maybe that would have kept him from getting into trouble," admonished the judge.

The attitude of the youngster who steals is often "if I don't have it, I will take it." This leads to theft of parts off stolen cars to use in dressing up an older car. It leads to theft of motorcycles because of a yen to own one. Or it may lead to stealing and selling articles to acquire other desired pieces. Young people are only trying to walk between the raindrops when they feel they will not be caught. The water gets deeper and deeper as thefts continue. Soon they are over their heads.

Auto thefts are common. The inexperienced, unlicensed youth steals a car. A wrecked car is often the end product, caused by reckless driving. Or, by pushing the car over an embankment. It may be the result of stripping the car to use or to sell the parts. It may be the result of burning the motor out. The property owner finds himself not only with a financial loss but with all the accompanying inconveniences. Hours are spent getting estimates, dealing with insurance companies, and hassling over other details. The price of personal inconvenience cannot be tagged.

Vandalism is often the companion of breaking and entering and burglary. Young offenders go from room to room destroying furniture, marking walls, ruining floor coverings. Clothing, books, and personal articles are demolished. Irreplaceable family treasures are destroyed. Fires are set. Understandably, home owners are overwhelmed with grief. Even monetarily, insurance will cover just so much. It can never heal the psychological damage of the one who has gone through such an experience.

Fear often grips the heart of the home owner returning to such a scene. Written on the walls are threats: "If the police get me, I will get you!" The anguish of finding the results of one's hard work destroyed so needlessly can only be understood fully by those who have personally experienced the trauma.

Although it is not necessarily true that such actions are committed by a group, at times groups of four or five young people band together to get their thrills from such activity. Going from home to home, perhaps in different cities, they totally destroy the interior. Pictures of the damage are indescribable. It is difficult to understand such irrational behavior. In a court hearing involving five young people, their movement from county to county was easily traced — the pattern was clearly recognizable. They had located and entered homes where the occupants were either working or vacationing.

Three young brothers, the oldest eleven, committed over forty home burglaries in addition to two auto thefts. They gave as their reason: "it was easy." Father worked a shift and a half. Mother was found by the investigation to be as dependent upon the boys as they were on her. Because her permissiveness was destructive, the boys had to be removed from the home, with instruction from the court: "no visitation with the boys for at least sixty days." Well-meaning parents, but inadequate.

A group of high school boys, accompanied by two junior high youngsters, went on a vandalism spree. When they were through, they had done over ten thousand dollars of damage to three schools. Stealing a car from one of the schools, they left the city, but were later apprehended. The most sickening act of their spree was the stomping to death of animals kept in the science rooms of one of the schools. "It was just a game," one of them explained. Defensive parents of two of the boys demanded they be accorded their rights to return to school.

Many parents are irresponsible in dealing with theft. They may ignore goods for which they cannot account. Or in some cases, the parents are found to be actively participating in the thefts. The participation may be passive — allowing the youngster to stash things away in the home. Or it may be active — there have been hearings where parents were using children to carry out their own planned burglaries. And some parents just do not classify stealing as being wrong. One parent actually stated in court: "When I was a kid, I took things too. I don't see that it is so bad!" The judge replied, "Then it is understandable why your son is a thief."

On the other hand, there are parents who do believe stealing is wrong and are supportive in carrying out correctional measures proposed by the court. Such parents are usually shocked, showing heart-felt grief and genuine concern.

The parents' attitudes will affect the child's attitude in setting goals for his own rehabilitation. The story of Mike illustrates the importance of attitudes — both of parents and children.

MIKE . . .

"Look how smart I am."

Mike's blond hair looked especially curly today. His father kept it manishly styled and cut. Mike was proud of his hair, but then Mike was a very proud twelve year old. He expressed this in many ways in conversation. He knew he had superior ability. He was a leader. His quick mind allowed him the advantage over the majority of adults who worked with him. He was manipulative, argumentative, and at times arrogantly defiant. He exhibited unusual skill in presenting his opinion in such a way that the listener could easily be persuaded, or could easily become angry with him. Any conversation with Mike became a wit-matching game. He thrived on this. Having his own way was almost an obsession with him. It was not obtaining the end product that was important to him, but winning the argument. He would actually gloat over his victory in later conversation by discussing his strategy and laughing over the experience.

This very strong, self-willed seventh grader was the adoptive son of parents who wanted so sincerely to do the right thing and show love at all times that they never realized or learned the secret of consistent discipline as a necessary ingredient of parental love. Mike took advantage of this. He recognized their lack of consistency, their lack of agreement in dealing with him, the lack of structure, the lack of well-defined reasonable limitations. He was aware of his own manipulative skill in wearing one or the other, or both, down. Although at times his father became so angry he used his belt on him, Mike took it in stride and knew his father would repent and buy him the trail bike or racing boat he had argued for. And it always happened just as Mike predicted.

Mike hated authority and control. He felt capable of self-management. Feeling superior to the adults attempting to manage him, he did as he pleased and relied upon his skillful manipulative ability to get him off the hook. It did not bother him that to accomplish his purposes he resorted to lying and other dishonest methods. That was just a part of winning.

Little wonder Mike's expression showed extreme aggravation and displeasure. He sat at his assigned position in the court room, his short, stocky frame upright, his lips taut, with a rigidity which suggested that he was about to become involved in the first combat in which he was not totally confident of winning. Mike was about to face the judge of the juvenile court, charged with burglarizing several homes in the area in which he lived.

According to the investigation, Mike with two friends entered the homes to take specific articles, such as parts for his bike or boat, and money. Extensive vandalism had also taken place.

The probation officer's report indicated that Mike's parents felt he had been influenced by his companions. Mike allowed this opinion to be used in his defense. The report indicated much planning, including staking out the area to determine the time schedule of the residents of the homes.

Included with the probation officer's report was a comprehensive psychological evaluation. This evaluation confirmed the fact of Mike's superior ability, but pointed out his resistance to authority and controls, his defiant and hostile attitude toward authority figures, strong self-will, manipulative skills, lack of interest in school, poor grades. The test also revealed a negative attitude toward his parents, the confusion and turmoil in the home, and his disregard for right and wrong. Mike was characterized by the psychologist as having one goal in life — getting his own way. He was also characterized as undisciplined and in need of firm, consistent guidelines which were reasonable, but which, if violated, carried reasonable consequences. The psychologist strongly recommended that Mike be held accountable for his actions, be ordered to follow rigid rules of probation, and undergo psychological counseling with his parents.

In conversation with his parents prior to entering the court room, Mike had lashed out at them, blaming them for his problems, and in angry tones demanded "get me out of this — you can if you want to — but I know you don't want to. You would like to see them punish me — send me up — well, just go ahead. You'll be sorry!"

His parents sat, confused, feeling guilty and concerned. The probation officer took his seat. Leaning toward Mike, he attempted to reassure him. The response he received from the boy was "just forget it. You are just like my folks. You don't care. I don't need you either."

"Please rise!"

The judge entered the room. His eyes were squarely focused on the blond twelve year old who stood rigidly before him. As the judge scrutinized him momentarily, Mike's shoulders sagged and he appeared relieved to take his seat at the clerk's directive. He lowered his head, and his facial expression indicated he knew he had at last entered a combat zone in which he was not superior.

The judge spoke:

"Now, let's get one thing straight. I have read your file. You have been allowed to do as you please. You have manipulated, you have harrassed. You have resorted to any means you felt necessary to have your way and you are smart enough to see where it got you. I would suggest that you not pull any of your shenanigans in this court room, that you sit up straight, and when I ask a question your answer is to be 'yes sir' and 'no sir.' Is that clear?"

"Yes, sir!" replied Mike.

"Very well." He turned to the probation officer. "Mr. Black, give me your report."

The probation officer went through the charge. He then began to outline for the court the premeditated plans of action. Following this, Mr. Black reiterated to the court his personal investigation of the incidents, including his work with Mike and his parents.

"Your Honor," began Mr. Black, "this is Mike's first time to be brought to the attention of the court. But in working with him and the parents, I am convinced we have a young man who will continue to be in very serious trouble if he does not begin to realize what he is doing to himself. I am hoping he is smart enough to see this. I don't feel we will have much difficulty here today. If Mike is allowed to return to the community, I hope he will be smart enough to understand that his arrogance, defiance of authority, and manipulation of his parents will have to stop. There is another thing I want to call to the court's attention. Mike indicates he feels every one else is stupid by his standards, but then he attempts to blame others for his actions. I have tried to point out to him that this is quite contradictory in content. Sometimes he comes on in a way which says 'look how smart I am. See what I can do. I can outwit my parents, my teachers.' But then when the pressure is on, he wants to appear as a little twelve year old who is led astray!"

Mike turned on the probation officer. "Don't call me stupid. You are trying to send me up! You don't like me!"

"Mike! Turn around here. One more outburst and you will go back to your cell. Your behavior just now indicates your immaturity and your need for help. Are you denying your part in these burglaries and in the vandalism? Are you going to tell me you were forced to take part against your will?" said the judge.

"No, sir," was the reply.

"Then, tell me what happened, and I want the truth. There is one thing I will not tolerate, and that is a lie. So think! But I want the whole truth."

Haltingly, Mike began. He gave an accounting of "the plan" he devised for a series of burglaries which he felt would never leave evidence of his involvement. He told of masterminding the plan, placing friends on stake-outs to observe time-scheduling patterns, of casing the homes to get an idea of articles he could use and of being especially interested in obtaining money with which he could purchase additional items.

"Then it was your plan, your idea," said the judge.

"They don't know enough about anything ... they wouldn't have known how to work it ..." Mike blurted out. A look of disbelief as to what he had said came over his face! "I mean ...."

"I know what you mean," said the judge. "It is perfectly clear."

Mike sat, head down. He had demonstrated his true attitude once again — in court. Someone in authority, older, much wiser, and willing to assume the responsibility for the outcome of the court hearing was in complete control, and Mike realized it. The realization appeared to shatter him. He had reached the point, at least for the purposes of this hearing, where he knew he could not match wits, manipulate, harrass, or coerce. He knew he would be evaluated on his own merits, and that he would be held accountable for his actions.

"Mr. and Mrs. Prince, your son is in trouble," the judge said to the parents. "I don't mean just burglary and vandalism, although that is serious. I mean in attitude, in his approach to life, himself, and others. I think you will have to share in this. Whether you are aware of it or not, you have turned being good and showing love into total emotional and moral destruction. You can't let a twelve year old do as he pleases. You need to be parents — not just two people who provide him with everything he wants and give in to his every whim. You can see where it leads! Quit blaming others. Get yourselves straightened out. Am I right?"

"Your Honor," Mr. Prince began, "you are right. We will do whatever the court says to try to straighten things out. We don't want our boy to be a criminal. We would like to take him home and see if we can do better."

"I'm not sure that is what Mike needs," said the judge. "He needs a firm hand, and I am not so sure you are ready to supply that."

"We are, Your Honor," the father replied.

Mike's mother sat with tears streaming down her face.

"Mrs. Prince, what are your feelings in this?" the judge inquired.

Mrs. Prince raised her head. She wiped her eyes. "Your Honor, I am too easy with him. His dad reasons, then gets worn down and angry. Then he uses a belt, but later gives in. I know we have to change. I would like to try."

The judge turned to the probation officer.

"I would recommend strict probation, Your Honor. If it doesn't work, Mike will be before this court again. He knows that. I guess the choice will be his."

"I'm going to commit you to the Department of Institutions, Mike —" the judge paused.

Mike's head shot up. A look of dismay covered his face. He stared at the judge. Moments seemed like hours as the stern eyes of the judge locked with those of the shocked twelve year old. Gradually Mike relaxed and slumped down in the chair with head bowed in resignation.

"What do you think of that?" asked the judge.

"I guess I have it coming," said Mike.

"I am going to suspend the commitment and send you home under strict probation ..." the judge began again.

Mike raised his head. A look of hope and relief came over his face.

"But if you violate these rules to the extent your probation officer feels you need to come before me again, you'd better pack your bags. I keep my promise and I can promise you that you will be committed. You and your family are to have counseling help. You will also report to your probation officer as directed. You will have a curfew, bring your grades up, obey your parents, and stay out of trouble. As these folks work with you, remember that if you come before me again you will be committed. Do you understand?"

"Yes, sir!" replied Mike.

The court hearing was concluded. Mike was smiling. His parents went to his side. Mike's comment to his parents was "you guys were no help!"

His mother stepped back in disbelief. His father took a step toward Mike and the probation officer intervened.

"Young man," he addressed Mike, "you came just that close. You had better wise up. Perhaps I had better ask the judge to change his decision."

"No, sir, I'll cooperate," promised Mike.

"Come with me," the probation officer said to Mike and his parents. "I want to introduce you to the one who will be working with you and assisting the court. She lives near you. I think she can do the job the judge wants done. He wants you, as a family, to report to someone each week — someone who would not let you do as you please, Mike, and someone, Mr. and Mrs. Prince, who can help you in working together effectively as parents with your son."

I was that someone the court asked to work with Mike and his parents. During the time I had worked with the court staff, I had become well acquainted with the expectations of the court. Mike and his parents lived in the country very near my home. Mr. Prince worked long hours, making it necessary for appointments to be scheduled with the family during the evening or on a week-end. Mr. and Mrs. Prince seemed happy with the arrangement. Mike had no recourse. The first appointment was set, and at this conference I was to see Mike alone. I shall never forget that session.

Mike informed me as soon as he sat down that he was all right and the world was all wrong. He did this as only Mike could do. I heard, in great detail, how stupid the teachers were, how unnecessary it was to take required subjects, how easy the work really was but just to "show them," he would not waste his time studying. I heard how incompetent his parents were, how unfair they were in their judgments, how unjust the court was, and had it not been that he might have been sent to the Department of Institutions he would have "told that judge a thing or two." I also understood quite emphatically that the only reason he had to report to me was so that I could be a squealer and send him back to the court. I heard a long, lengthy dissertation on how his rights had been infringed upon, how undeniably accurate his evaluations and interpretations of all life experiences really were, how he was going to prove to everyone that his way was right and that ultimately he would be the rich, controlling authority figure, doing just as he pleased. Throughout all of this there was no indication of even a hint of responsibility toward any other person, nor to the court. I listened. I continued to listen as Mike pointed out his own virtues. Obviously Mike felt he needed no one. After about an hour, I felt I had heard enough.

"Are you through, Mike?" I asked. He looked startled. "Because I think I know your problem. You need the Lord."

"THE LORD! What are you talking about? I don't need anybody — much less HIM! So don't give me that. I don't go to church and I am not the religious type!"

"That is obvious, Mike. But you do need the Lord, and I want you to know that my goal will be to get you to the place where you will come to realize this. Now, if you don't want to work with me, I will call your probation officer and ask that he have you see someone else. Because, you see, I am not paid by the court to see you. I am seeing you because I want to, but that feeling has to be mutual. If you are going to see me again, it will have to be at your choice. I want you to know that you do not have to. But, if you do, you may be sure that I will be in control, and you will do as I say. You will be accountable to me. Is that clear? Now, what is your decision?"

Mike sat. He started to say something, sputtered, and apparently thought better of it. He mumbled "man" a few times, sat a little longer, and then said, "When do you want me to come back?"

"I'll come to your home on Friday evening, Mike. I want to see you with your parents. We are going to discuss ways for you to gain a better understanding of yourselves and one another. We are going to set some guidelines for your behavior. I want a progress report from your teachers. I will ask your mother to get that. We are going to establish some study habits. In short, Mike, we are going to completely rearrange your schedule to include consideration and concern for others, and also to include responsibility for yourself and for your actions at all times."

Mike looked at me in disbelief. He did not say a word. His mother arrived to take him home. She honked the horn. Mike rose to go. "See you Friday," he said as he went out the door.

Friday came. When I arrived at the Prince home, the evening meal had just been finished. Mr. Prince was having an after-dinner glass of wine. There was evidence of what appeared to have been a nice spaghetti dinner. There was also evidence that the family was just a little up-tight for this first visit in the home. Mr. Prince offered me some wine. When I declined he said, "Oh, excuse me. Mike said you were religious ...." I felt it necessary to explain to the parents my personal position in working with Mike and with them. The same opportunity to withdraw from further sessions was offered them. Mrs. Prince wished to continue, saying, "I think you care about Mike as a person, and I think you will be honest with us. I know we have a lot to learn, and I know you won't tell us wrong. Maybe we don't all believe alike, but I like what you believe. It is not my way, but I trust your way. We would like to continue." Mr. Prince agreed. All eyes turned to Mike. "Sure, let's get started."

That evening was long. I heard of their disagreements in child-rearing practices. I heard accusations by Mike toward his parents, of each parent toward Mike and toward one another. There was an undercurrent of bitterness. There were money problems, which Mrs. Prince felt should never have happened.

And in the middle of all of this a five foot one inch twelve year old was taking it all in and using it to his own distinct advantage. He had been allowed to be the center of it all and was enjoying it. In the many confrontations between child and parents, the parents suffered many guilt feelings and to assuage their guilt allowed Mike to manipulate them and get all of the material benefits he desired. He was smart enough to lay the trap for them.

That evening he set them up on several occasions. Then, very cunningly, he diverted the conversation to a racing hull that he wanted. He made them feel so guilty! Mrs. Prince stated that Mike had been told he could have the racing hull if he would take good care of the yard that year. She told of the sloppy job he had done in the distribution of some ground bark, of his hurried motions in doing the work, of his leaving the yard without completing the job or telling her where he was going. Mike explained he had gone down to the beach to watch as some "more fortunate" kids were enjoying their racing hulls. He stated the summer season was so short and he felt he should be allowed to have the racer NOW and pay for it later. And unbelievably, the father agreed. Mike was jubilant, his mother was overwhelmed, and I was disgusted. We were able to turn the situation around by setting up a repayment plan for Mike which carried with it the condition that if the work were not done and done well, there would be no using of the racing hull, and I would enforce the rule if the parents found he disobeyed them. The penalty for the illegal use of the racer for one hour would be one week-end in detention. (Mike challenged me on this one, and although it was difficult to do, I placed him in detention for one week-end — unfortunately one of the warmest, nicest week-ends of the summer! There was no second time.)

I saw Mike at least once a week for the next two years. More often some weeks. His mother would call frantically when there would be some confrontation with him. Mike would fight us all for awhile, but eventually I could reason with him, and he would agree that he could have managed better. At times Mike would call, wanting me to tell his parents they *had* to do something he thought was best. It was necessary, on occasion, to stand toe to toe with Mike and let him know he could not have his way. He made gains. His grades went up. He went to Sunday school and church with us on occasion. His mother also attended a few times. His father would never attend. He had other things to do.

During these two years Mike and I had some interesting discussions about the things of God. Mike became more and more open and brought up the subject more often. He seemed genuinely interested, and it was obvious he knew he had a need. But during those two years I did not feel he ever reached a point of truly receiving Christ as Savior. Neither did his parents.

After two years I felt I had done all I could for Mike. His parents were with him in our home on that evening. I spoke very frankly with them as we reviewed the record. Together we agreed that all had been said that could be said, that it really was time they lived as a family without any outside influence. A great dependence had begun to develop that was not really healthy. It was clear to the family that I felt there was no solution to their problems outside of Christ. It was also clear to them that this would have to be their decision, and in no way were they accountable to me for their decision regarding a personal relationship with the Lord. The scheduled sessions were terminated, but I assured Mike and his parents that should there come time when I could be of help, they were welcome to call.

Mike was in high school when I heard from him again. He was in detention, accused of taking coins from a home in the area. He asked to see me. When I spoke with him, I knew he was telling me the truth when he told me he did not take the coins. He had been implicated by boys who had been involved, but he was not guilty of theft. I asked the probation officer for permission to take him home, indicating I would be responsible should the investigation prove he was guilty. He was cleared. His parents were very grateful, as was Mike. Mike could at last show and express appreciation. I was overjoyed! I encouraged Mike once again to use his good ability, to make something of himself, and to consider his need of the Lord. Mike told me he really had made a decision, but that he did not know how to express it. He seemed to feel reassured when I told him this was between him and the Lord, that it was not necessary that he express his feeling just so to me. I pointed out his need to read God's Word and to locate himself in a Bible teaching church where he could grow. This did not appeal to Mike. I left him at that point.

When Mike was a junior in high school, I received a call from his home, made by a deputy sheriff. Mike's mother had called for assistance when he came home from school smelling of glue and acting strangely. He reportedly attempted to assault her. She ran from the home and called for help. The deputy said Mike had asked him to call me. The deputy wanted to know what he should do, since Mike said he was under my supervision. I could see through that! I told the deputy he should do with Mike as he would any other young person. Mike went to jail.

I visited a remorseful Mike at the detention hall. He told me he had become curious about the effects glue would have on him and he had tried it on two or three occasions. It was true he had not been in trouble for quite awhile, but to sniff glue! I discussed this with him very seriously, pointing out the personal injury he could cause himself. When Mike felt he would be the one to lose, he could straighten out, and he did so in this instance. But because he had been driving under the influence of the glue, his license was taken for six months. He came to see me often during that time, admittedly to convince me I should intercede regarding the license. I did not. But I took advantage of these times to listen to Mike and to observe his growth in some areas. He was doing better in school and would be graduating within the year. He had no plans for college. "I want to have some fun for awhile." At the end of the six month period, Mike's license was returned. I did not hear from him again for almost three years.

The door bell rang. There stood Mike. It was as though he had stopped by just last week. He was the same old Mike, infectious grin and all. "Hi. I just stopped by. I need to talk to you about something."

I invited him in. We had friends in for dinner. Introductions were made, and we asked Mike to join us at the table. He did, chatting away in his own friendly fashion. Mike never met a stranger.

"I am joining the Marines," he announced, "and I need your help. When they investigate my record, I want to know what they will do about my record at the Hall. They will ask me whether I have ever been arrested. What shall I tell them?"

"Tell them the truth, Mike. Your juvenile record is just that. You have not faced a formal charge since you were in the seventh grade. That was a long time ago. Now you have made a decision to go into the Marines. But before you go, there is another decision you must make," I replied.

"I know," Mike answered. "I knew I had to come here tonight because I knew I had to make that decision. I did make a decision a long time ago, but I have held out ... and now I want to be sure...."

The young couple visiting with us that evening had recently been told their little son was terminally ill. They were radiant as they spoke with Mike regarding God's faithfulness in meeting their need and shared with him the difference Christ made in their lives. Mike was overwhelmed by their faith in the midst of their sorrow. He saw the reality of living faith in the lives of this family.

We had prayer. Mike prayed, asking Christ to be his Savior. "I'll be in church Sunday and I will bring my mom. She needs the Lord, too."

Sunday morning he was there with his mom. When the invitation to pray at the altar was given, Mike took his mother's hand and said, "You come with me, too. You need the Lord." Together they went down the aisle. Mike stood proudly beside his mother and looked at the congregation as though to say "I've won again!" And indeed he had.

Mike went into the Marines as he had planned. He married shortly after that. His mother continued to attend church. She sang in the choir, and was involved in a Bible study class. She began to grow. Mike's father had left the home before Mike entered the Marines. He has since returned to the home, but has not attended church. But, as Mike says, "The Lord will get him one day . . . just like He did me."

Mike has since returned to the community from his hitch in the Marines. He still talks about how rebellious he was, what a brat he was, how pig-headed and self-willed he was, but how underneath it all he knew the answer to his problems then, and to any problem he will ever encounter. That answer is the Lord!

Chapter 3

Often a youngster is involved in various categories of crimes, some of them interrelated.

An act of delinquency frequently before the court is assault. Assaults are on the increase. Young people are smashing their peers and adults. When they find themselves unable to verbally control a situation, they resort to explosive outbursts — severe beatings requiring hospitalization, use of knives to settle differences, or even a gun that has been carried to school.

One of the most bizarre assault cases brought to the attention of the court involved four girls against one. It seems the one girl had either intentionally or unintentionally been friendly with the boy friend of one of the four. She was taken from the school building to a wooded area nearby where she was harrassed, intimidated, and threatened. A knife was used to cut off her hair. In emotional shock, she required medical care. The court hearing revealed a variety of attitudes. One of the girls felt her drastic solution to the problem had been justified. Another went along with her friend. The other two were less involved, but they were equally as guilty. They were there! They did nothing to stop the action! The court ordered the four to pay the medical expenses of the victim. Can money compensate for such psychological damage?

Adults, too, are victims of assaults. Teachers are often threatened and assaulted. In fact, teachers actually fear retaliation when reporting some children to the police or to school administrators. It is safer to turn one's back than to get involved. Old women are fearful of going to the grocery store. Purse snatching attempts often result in physical harm to the victim, even heart attacks.

Armed robbery attempts have ended in homicide. In such cases, the youthful offender is before the juvenile court on a declination petition. Young people do carry weapons. When placed in a threatening situation, they use them.

The possession and use of alcohol has been declared by some to be replacing drug abuse. This may be true in some parts of the country. The teenage alcoholic is not uncommon. Young people of junior high age admit the need of that drink to be able to face the day at school. Because of the anticipation of whatever exhilarated feeling accompanies drink, they are setting themselves up for years of bondage. Liquor is easily obtained even in the home. One parent indicated "we take a sensible approach to alcohol. We have our cocktail before dinner, wine with our meals ...." A parent with such an attitude may not be so distraught over having a teenage alcoholic in the home. Young people can also buy their booze. Money floats freely in the pockets of many children today. If the youthful consumer is not able to make the purchase, he can easily secure this favor from an older person. A sixpack is often a welcome pay off for some adult who also feels the need for a lift from the bottle.

Even though the use of alcohol is on the rise, drug abuse is still going strong among youth. Many have graduated from marijuana and are now mainlining — shooting heroin. That deadly white powder has produced emaciated, incapacitated victims — still holding on, believing they can kick the habit!

Young people will resort to any delinquent act to obtain money to support the habit. Prostitution, armed robbery, burglary — wherever the possibility for obtaining money exists, they are there. They steal from parents. They steal from friends! They show up in court as total wrecks. One of the saddest pictures in the court room is that of an emaciated youth, needle marks visible on his arms, sitting staring into space, incoherent, not understanding, unable to explain his plight. So often brilliant young people, with high native ability, perhaps star athletes, appear in court. Their bodies carry the scars of drug abuse. Weight loss from 180 pounds to under 100 pounds is not uncommon. Once beautiful girls are haggard and drawn — thirteen going on thirty! A wasted life. There is often no turning back at this point. Psychiatrists called in to examine, evaluate, and recommend often come back with the answer: "It is too late!"

Danny was one of those involved in drugs and accompanying criminal actions.

DANNY . . .

"Was love enough?"

Danny scooted forward to the edge of his chair in an effort to sit with his feet firmly placed on the floor. This appeared to be very important to him — as though he were determined to give an appearance of strength, not only to those in the court room, but also to the judge who would be entering shortly and to whom Danny would be accountable regarding the charge. Satisfied finally with his seating arrangement, Danny sat with an expression on his face which suggested he was thinking "I'm going to beat this one." Just another incident to deal with — let's get on with it!

This was a most unusual case. Though only a sixth grader, Danny had been known to the court for some time. His first arrest had occurred the year before when he had threatened another child with a knife. Danny had taken the knife to school that day with the intent of robbing the bus driver on the return trip. One of the children became aware of these facts and reported to the teacher. When Danny found out, he threatened to use the knife on his classmate. Following a few days in detention, he was released to his mother. Now he found himself once again involved in a very serious delinquency.

The father was a retired army man, but because of a very large family of twelve children, it was necessary that he work long hours. Mrs. Saxon also worked in order to supplement the family income. Because of his duties in the service and now on the job, Mr. Saxon left the rearing of the children to his wife. There was much love in the home, but little time for parental guidance and direction. In reality the older children were rearing the younger ones. Each child had household responsibilities. Mrs. Saxon felt they were capable and trustworthy. But in the absence of parent figures, supervision of younger came from older children. At times, there were physical clashes between Danny and one of the other children.

Mrs. Saxon recognized her inability to cope with Danny's problems early. She knew they were beyond the scope of her understanding and ability without some assistance. Danny and his mother were seen by the school social worker for a period of time. However, it was clear that Danny had deeper problems. His mother made arrangements for him to be seen by a psychiatrist at the army medical center. The diagnosis confirmed deep-seated emotional problems. Recommendations for dealing with these were made to the school staff, but Danny failed to adjust.

By the time he was in sixth grade, Danny had been suspended once, taken from the school by juvenile authorities on two occasions, and questioned on another occasion regarding delinquent acts. He was extremely disruptive in class, interacting with other children in a way that threw the room into turmoil and created an atmosphere hardly conducive to learning. His behavior on the bus was so deplorable that he was not allowed to ride. At home he worried his mother by staying out until five or six in the morning. Overwhelmed with the responsibilities of a large family, Mrs. Saxon sought desperately for help. Despite the home, community, and school efforts Danny went his way.

A warm likeable child but with a hot temper, he was always ready to fight! When so motivated, he could interact positively with others and could make friends easily. But as a result of his lack of self-control, he could not keep his friends. He was a youngster with average ability, but due to excessive absenteeism, behavioral problems, and poor self-image, he was not achieving.

At school he was often cast as "bad," as a result of his incorrigible behavior. Danny acted the class clown or misbehaved to gain the attention of his peers and teachers. One of his many strengths was that he seemed to want and need a positive relationship with an adult. When this was offered in a group, however, he could not handle it. Consequently, a one to one relationship was necessary if gains were to be made — an impossible demand in a classroom of children. As a result, any classroom that listed Danny on the rolls became a battleground. Without intending to do so, his parents also reinforced his behavior by characterizing him as "bad."

As his self-concept became more and more damaged, Danny became more aggressive, hostile, and difficult to manage at home, at school, and in the community. Danny seemed to crave belonging and acceptance as a person. He seemed to be seeking for someone to depend on. Because of his anxiety, fearfulness, and depression, he vacillated between somewhat rigid controls for himself to very lax standards of conduct. But Danny always left the impression that underneath he really wanted to meet the expectations of home, school, and community. However, the impulsive, troubled, angry feelings would invariably win out and he would find himself in difficulty again. Working with Danny was like working with two different people, depending on the mood of the moment.

Mrs. Saxon sat, eyes never moving from her son. The distressed, anxious expression on her face carried with it a cry for help. She so loved Danny! In her love she knew she needed direction in working with him. In reality she had three jobs — trying to be mother to eleven other children, working full time, and attempting to meet Danny's needs. She could not possibly give full attention to any one of these. This did not lessen the pain she felt as a mother. Mrs. Saxon frankly admitted she did not know how to reach Danny.

Danny was now before the court, charged with auto theft. In reviewing the case with the probation officer, it was learned Danny had previously been arrested for auto theft, held for a few days, and then released to his mother. Following his release, he involved himself in three more auto thefts. This made a court hearing mandatory. The probation officer believed Danny needed to hear from the judge what the ultimate consequences of such acts would be if he continued in his delinquent behavior pattern.

In a review of the current situation with Mrs. Saxon and Danny prior to the hearing, it was evident he was not remorseful. He seemed aggravated with the inconvenience of detention and a court hearing. His only concern seemed to be "how long do I have to stay here?" Mrs. Saxon pleaded with him to change, to understand the seriousness of his actions: "Danny, I've brought you up good ... we love you ... we have provided good things for you ... you are only twelve and not old enough to drive a car ... God will deal with you if you don't straighten up...." To all of this Danny responded, as usual, with a blank stare and an impatient shifting of his feet and body. Conversing, if that is the appropriate term, with Danny left one with a deep appreciation of the frustration others experienced in working with him. There seemed to be no breaking through.

"Danny," the probation officer was speaking to him, "be sure to stand when the judge enters the court room. Remain standing until he is seated. I want you to answer his questions. Judge Spears is a nice person and he will want to ask you some questions. Speak up so he can hear you and answer, won't you?"

Danny did not respond.

With a totally frustrated look, the probation officer began to shuffle the papers before him. As he turned from Danny to the papers, it was evident he did not know what recommendation to give the court.

"Don't fret, Mr. Ogden. You have done your best ... it will be all right," said Danny's mother as she attempted to reassure him.

"Please rise!"

The court clerk had entered the room, and following her was His Honor, Judge Spears. Danny reluctantly stood, but only after the probation officer had begun to move to his side. He refrained from looking at the judge and as he sat down, he lowered his head and sat back in his chair, his feet well off the floor and his shoulders sagging. Danny looked so small! What had gone wrong that such a little boy had become so involved in such serious delinquent acts? As I glanced from face to face, I saw the same question on each face — where do we go from here? Can the problem be met head on? Is there a plan which will divert this child from the pattern of behavior he is exhibiting, or is this going to be a child who will continue breaking the rules and the laws even into adulthood?

"Danny, I am Judge Spears," began His Honor. "I have read your file and the petition filed against you. As I now have the opportunity to observe you, I must confess I am overwhelmed at your size and over-all appearance. It is difficult to reconcile my impression of you with the acts you have committed. You did take the cars, did you not?" Danny did not answer. Judge Spears waited a few moments. Then, as though to allow Danny an opportunity to grasp the situation, he turned to the probation officer. "Mr. Ogden, will you give me the background of this case and your recommendation, please."

The probation officer began to unfold for the judge a report of his work with Danny. He spoke of Danny's first arrests for threatening to use a knife on a classmate; he told of the problems in the home, the concern of the family, the multiple school-related problems. He mentioned the interaction of social agencies with the family, of assistance from various specialized staff from the schools, of the report of the psychiatrist indicating Danny had some rather deep-seated emotional problems. Mr. Ogden also referred to the earlier arrest on auto theft, the boy's release, and subsequent theft of three additional autos, making it necessary for the court hearing to be held. "Your Honor, I have no recommendation. I will have to ask the court, in its wisdom, to evaluate the facts and make a disposition of the case. I am baffled. You see Danny today as I have seen him for the past several days. He is uncommunicative. I do not know how he feels. I do know that his parents want him home, and they would like to have some assistance as recommended by the court. I am concerned about Danny. He really troubles me. I know that if he does not realize the seriousness of this, and make some changes, we will see him again, soon."

"Do you think you could look up, Danny, and speak with me?" asked Judge Spears. "I know you are afraid...."

"I am not," said Danny. Momentarily, he faced the judge. For that moment, he challenged the court with his hostile outburst, but just as quickly, he lowered his head and refused to look up again.

"Well, if you are not, Danny, you should be," said Judge Spears. "This is very serious, and I want you to know that. I cannot let you go around threatening others, stealing cars, acting out in school, and giving your parents and brothers and sisters a bad time. You understand that, don't you?"

"Yes," mumbled Danny.

"Well, what do you think I should do with you? You don't want me to keep you locked up, do you?"

Danny shook his head negatively.

"You better help me, then. We have to do something and do it fast. What are your feelings in this, Mrs. Saxon?"

"Your Honor, sir, I wish I knew. We have to help," agreed Mrs. Saxon, "but I have tried everything. If you will tell me what to do, I will do it. I do want him home. We all do. It breaks my heart to think he might not be able to come home, but I understand this is serious."

"Danny, do you have anything to say?" asked the judge.

Danny's silence was the judge's answer.

"If you were not so young, Danny, I would commit you to the Department of Institutions, but I hate to do that to a twelve year old. I'm going to say some things to you and I want you to listen. You are headed for trouble with a capital T. If you continue the way you are going, you will spend most of your life in jail. I think you have emotional problems that you are not able to cope with. I tell you what my plan is. I *am* going to commit you to the Department of Institutions. But I am going to suspend that commitment and place you on strict rules of probation which you must follow or you will be returned here." The judge paused. Danny continued to look down, as though he were totally detached from the scene. His body was immobile, not even an eyelash moved.

"Mr Ogden, I want you to work out, with Mrs. Saxon, a plan for some psychiatric counseling for this boy. He needs some help. This is to include family counseling as well. I have no doubt but what this child is deeply loved, but in this situation, I don't think that is enough. It is interesting that in the same home it is possible for two children to respond differently. One has greater needs — needs that cannot be met in the normal interaction of family living. This may be simply because parents do not have a true understanding of the need, or perhaps because they are not equipped with resources to meet this need. I want Danny on a curfew and I want his attendance to improve at school. I want no more of this threatening, fighting, or any other kind of disruption in the school, and I want him to begin to produce better grades. Now, Mr. Ogden, I address this to you, and to Mrs. Saxon, because for whatever reason, I cannot get through to Danny. If he were older and acted this way, I would commit him. But I feel he deserves our support and effort in attempting to evaluate and meet his needs. Do you agree, Mrs. Saxon?"

"I do, Your Honor, and I thank you. If Danny will work with us, we will try — very hard."

"Mr. Ogden, will you get right on this?"

"Yes, Your Honor."

"Very well. Danny, go home. Obey your parents and do as Mr. Ogden tells you, and I don't want to see you here again. If I do, despite your age, I will have no choice but to commit you." Judge Spears rose and left the court room.

Mrs. Saxon was weeping as she thanked the probation officer. "I don't know ... I just don't know ... what are we going to do?"

Attempting to comfort her, Mr. Ogden assured her that he would assist her in making a referral to one of the mental health clinics, on the army base or in the community. He asked her to give him a call within a few days, stating he would direct her in her efforts to assist her son. Danny still sat, head down.

"You may go home now, Danny," said Mr. Ogden, "but I hope you heard the judge. I will see you again in a few days."

Danny rose and walked past his mother, the probation officer, and others in the room. He did not say a word. There was no hope in the expressions on the faces of those in the room.

As suspected, Danny was totally uncooperative in following through with any plan devised by the court. As the result of the busy schedule of the mother and the multiple cases assigned to the probation officer, Danny was not forced to receive the care he needed and very soon came to the attention of the police again. Within a few months, he was re-entered at the juvenile detention hall for loitering and possession of stolen property. A few days later, following his release, he was entered once again on a burglary charge. He was handled on an unofficial basis rather than taken before the judge again, and was sent home. Once again, an effort made to involve Danny in a counseling program failed.

Danny was now in junior high school. Within the year he had been in three different schools in an effort to assist in his adjustment. Danny was characterized as a "constant problem" by his principals. Because he became unmanageable in the school setting, he was suspended. The psychologist recommended that Danny remain out of school for a period of time to determine adjustment within the community, and that reentry to school be left to Danny's ability and desire to initiate such action. In examining his response to efforts to control him in the school setting, it was found that verbal discipline seemed to be very confusing to Danny. Danny did not fully understand the differences in behavior and the differences in punishment.

Within a month, Danny was asking to be returned to school. An effort was made to create an environment and a control system which he could understand and to which he could respond. He received a conditional transfer to another junior high school. He finished out the year there.

During the next few months he again became involved with the police and was referred to his probation officer for auto theft and possession of stolen property and larceny. He was released without facing the judge. In less than a month he was returned to the Hall for auto theft and once again released.

Although several months passed before Danny was involved in illegal activity in the community, he was having problems at school, and was suspended. The listed violations included failure to cooperate, horseplay in the halls, putting crayons on a hot radiator, failure to report for detention, misbehavior in class, disobedience and disrespect to teachers, fighting, smoking, and truancy. Following a conference at the district office, he was returned to school with the warning he would be out if he did not respond to rules and regulations. He did fairly well, but within a couple of months was arrested for armed robbery. Danny had been assigned a different probation officer by now, and so was brought before the judge.

The investigation revealed that Danny had become extensively involved in the use of drugs. He had violated every rule of probation, even though he had had the benefit of intensive supervision for several months. When Danny appeared in court, the action taken by the judge was inevitable.

"Danny, it is apparent to me you need more help than this court can provide. Your probation officer, Mrs. Timms, has attempted to work with you. The school people have attempted to work with you. Your parents have attempted to work with you. Your parents have attempted to work with you. You have had the advantage of counseling and of weekly visits with your probation officer. You seem determined to test the limits of this court. Not only are you using marijuana, but have resorted to totally destructive drugs. You are going to kill yourself if someone does not force you to behave. You leave me no alternative but to commit you to the Department of Institutions. I wish you well. But let me remind you, unless you help yourself, no one will be able to help you."

58/THE DELINQUENT CHILD

Danny made no response. Although his mother appeared tearful, she seemed relieved. She was weary, worn out in her efforts to find a solution. As she explained, "When he is home, he minds. When he leaves, I don't know what he will do. I just don't understand him."

The following year Danny returned to the community. He had spent his institutional stay, following transfer from the diagnostic center, in a forestry camp. He was now in high school. His parole counselor and he asked for a transfer from his resident school to a school across the city in order to be away from old friends. This was effected. Within a month, he was again truant. He was now living with his sister, and catching the bus at the appropriate time presented a problem. He asked for a transfer to a different high school. This was denied because he was taking an irresponsible approach to his problem.

Early in the next school year, Danny was residing in the home of his brother in a different part of town. He was now requesting an alternate plan to regular day school and a release at the end of the quarter to attend the high school completion program at the community college. He was granted the release. His plan to attend the high school completion program never materialized.

Time passed, and because Danny was not involved in a school program, I heard little of him until the following September. Danny was in court again, charged with armed robbery, but on a declination hearing with the petition requesting a transfer to adult status. The probation officer listed as his reasons for the request the seriousness of the charge, the fact Danny would be eighteen in three weeks, his numerous prior contacts with juvenile court, the need for protection of the community, the fact parole did not work for him, the fact he was alleged to be using heroin extensively, and the lack of a program for him in the juvenile system.

There was no discussion in juvenile court as to the facts surrounding the case against Danny. The charge was that he had committed an armed robbery and had beaten the store owner unmercifully with his pistol. Mrs. Saxon was truly burdened at this hearing. The attorney, appointed by the state to represent Danny, appealed to the court to allow him to remain within the jurisdiction of the juvenile court. The deputy prosecutor, representing the state, backed with a lengthy record, had a strong case for declination. Danny was transferred to adult status. His file was referred to the prosecutor's office where charges would be prepared and filed against him. Danny did not seem concerned.

Danny did not go to trial as an adult. He did not reach his eighteenth birthday. Danny died from an overdose of drugs just three days after the hearing transferring him to adult status.

I heard the story from his father and mother. Broken-hearted parents, still questioning months after Danny's death. Why wouldn't he listen? Why was he so different from the other children? Why was he so determined at times to do the right thing, and then go right out and get himself so involved?

As I was seated in the living room of Danny's parents, some eighteen months after his death, his parents shared some of their feelings.

"You know," began his father, "I think his big problem was that he started running around with the wrong bunch too young. He always went with the older guys. They would come around, ask him to go, and he would. He was easily led. He wanted to be liked. One thing that just about killed me was the fact that he took an eleven hundred dollar ring of mine, gave it to some dope dealer for drugs. That was on Wednesday before he died on Sunday night or early Monday morning. The day before he died, he asked me, 'Daddy, are you mad at me?' and I said, 'Shouldn't I be?' He was obedient at home, but when he went into the street he did as he pleased. He was hooked on heroin, and he took any street drug he could get his hands on. When he was in high school, he stole seven new automobiles and parked them over by the golf course. The law never did catch him. He would sell the parts, or trade for drugs.

"I never saw anyone live like he did," continued his father. "After he went in that store to rob that man, I asked him why he whipped the man with his pistol. You know what he said. 'Because he didn't have any money!' I just don't understand that. He was really hooked on drugs, and he was trying to get money for more. He would do anything to get drugs. School was not for him. When he came home from the institution, I thought he was coming out of it, but it didn't work. He was never disciplined, only with the mouth, never paddled. I think that was wrong. He didn't do any chores after school. The older kids worked hard, but he did nothing. He would help with the lawn sometimes. Maybe scrub the porch, but he didn't work like the older kids."

"He had lots of love, though," said Mrs. Saxon. "He obeyed when he was in the house, but he would go out when we went to sleep. I never paddled him, nor any of the kids. They are my honeys. I always felt I shouldn't give up, just keep showing my love and maybe he would change. It didn't happen."

"If I had it to do over again," said Mr. Saxon, "I know what I would do. I would not allow him to go around with older fellows. I would put my foot down. It was so much trouble if I wanted to discipline him, I just folded my arms and let it go. His mom was his buddy, and that just isn't good. Oh, sure, he minded here in the house. But when he was on the street, we didn't know what he was doing."

"On Saturday before he died," began his mother, "we had a big dinner here. All the kids were home. Danny seemed happy, ate a lot.

Everybody laughed, and had fun ... lots of love in our family, very close knit. I had a long conversation out in the yard with Danny. We talked about a lot of things. When we came in, he went to sleep watching TV, but then got up and went to bed. On Sunday after he got up he ate his breakfast. In the evening his dad and I went to a friend's home and he left while we were gone. The next morning we were having breakfast, it was early, I heard the sirens. Then I heard a loud knock on the door and this lady was there ... she said for me to come quick ... she thought Danny was dead ... I went, over there ... a few streets over ... the police were there ... they said he was dead. The lady told me what happened. Danny had gone to see his girl friend — the daughter of the lady who came for me — and he was watching TV. The girl's mother was vacuuming. He offered to help. She told him she would finish. He sat, watching TV. He was in the middle of a program when the others went to bed and left him to turn off the TV when he was through. He died there in the chair ... it tore us apart ... we are so close ... but we learned some lessons, and life has to go on ....

"It was a large funeral," continued the mother. "The man at the mortuary said it was the second largest they had ever had. His friends loved him ... he looked so nice ... his brother spent about three hundred dollars on clothes for him ... he liked nice clothes, and rings ... diamonds. His friends placed much of their jewelry in the casket ... he really looked nice ... real nice."

Danny is gone. Left behind is a gray-haired father, who has worked hard to take care of his family. Mother is also lonely without her son.

Mother expressed a deep faith in the Lord. She feels she has a personal relationship with Him. She says she knows that had Danny allowed the Lord to control his life, things would have been different, but she says she also left that up to Danny.

Oh, yes, before we leave this scene. The ring Danny stole from his father for the purpose of obtaining drugs was returned to the father by the pusher. His explanation: he just didn't have the heart to keep it after Danny's death. But he had the heart to take it and in return supply the drugs that took the life of a young man, just a few days short of his eighteenth birthday.

"We will never know all the facts," concluded his mother. She had walked outside with me. We were standing in the yard. "See that chair ... that is where we sat, just the night before he died ... we talked about three hours. I thought he really had it put together ... but he just couldn't leave the drugs alone. I sure do miss him. I loved him so much!"

Chapter 4

To a parent who is explaining how involved the family is in church activities, the judge responds: "It is not my intent to discuss the impact of religion in a person's life. This is a matter of personal choice. But I will say this: I fail to see the consistency in being an active church member and yet not being available for your children. It seems to me there is more to religion than that."

To the parent who is declaring he is not able to control his child or set into operation a successful plan for his child's life, the judge may declare: "Don't tell me what you can't do. Tell me what you can do! I am tired of hearing the negative side. You share this responsibility! This is your child. You helped make the mess. Then you come in here for the answer!"

To the parent who sat working with a thread of her sweater while her son was being adjudicated on a delinquency charge, the judge challenged: "It is plain to see where your interests are. You are not listening, much less hearing what is going on. I believe you want this child committed. In his best interests that will be the disposition. There is no help for him at home."

To the mother who indicated that had her husband known it was necessary, he would have been at the hearing, the judge intoned: "Do you mean to tell me a father needs someone to tell him it is necessary to be in court when he has a son here?"

She replied, "He has the feeling we have not had help from the court. Our boy really has not done anything wrong. We feel you are picking on him!" The answer of the judge to this cannot be adequately expressed. She knew she had been in court when he was through!

Juvenile court judges hold that a child is a part of a family unit. Interaction between parent and child is important. The parent cannot assume a role of non-involvement. He must become a part of his child's situation. He needs to be supportive and active throughout the procedure. In love, but in discriminating love, he wants his child home. He wants to work with him, to provide the proper guidance. He learns from his child's experience, and becomes a stronger person as a result. Despite the pronoun used, this incudes mothers. Children need two parents.

DON ...

"It takes more than a biological act."

Don moved slowly into the court room. Although he was well over six feet tall, he appeared small, bewildered, and for his seventeen years, very young. His probation officer followed him in, and placing a hand on his arm directed him to the chair which would seat him directly in front of the judge who would be entering shortly.

"Now, Don," began the probation officer, "don't be nervous. As I told you, Judge Robinson will be hearing your case. He is very easy to talk with. So feel free to speak up; say what you think. Remember, stand when the judge comes in. Now, turn around and say hello to your parents while you are waiting."

Don did not turn. He sat, looking directly ahead, head held high, hands clenched together, an anxious look on his face. He shifted his body, shuffled his feet a few times and then settled down in a stiff, almost statuesque position. He seemed to block out every person and everything in the court room as he kept his lonely vigil in anticipation of the judge's entry.

The probation officer took his seat to the back and right of Don. He sat, turning the typewritten pages he held in his hand as he came into the court room, apparently reviewing the facts of the case in preparation for his presentation to the court. He appeared intent, carefully examining the pages a second time, making notes as he read. Looking up, he paused and directed a comment to Don. "Relax, I am here. Do you have any questions, anything you want to discuss before we begin?" Don shook his head negatively, remaining in the same rigid position.

Mr. Langley, the probation officer, had held his position for fifteen years. Before coming to the juvenile court in this capacity, he had worked with various youth groups in the community. In his position as probation officer he had an opportunity to assist young people and to gain a deeper understanding of the uniqueness of the specific needs in each case.

In reviewing Don's case with the probation officer, it was learned that Don came from a home of comfortable means. His father had a responsible position with a large industrial firm. His mother had never worked outside the home, but she did have varied interests which took her away from home frequently. Don had two younger sisters. Although the family was not wealthy, money or material benefits was not a problem. The physical appearance of each family member seated in the court room attested to this fact.

In the earlier, struggling years there had been a strengthening cohesiveness in the family group of father, mother, and son. Even a leaning toward "religion and things of the church — we used to go all the time." But with promotions, prosperity, and progress came the falling away and the family, who at one time seemed to have a hunger for the things of the Lord, was swept up in the social whirl of job activities, entertainment, and clubs. Little by little, the fire went out, the Spirit was quenched. Two daughters were later added to the family. They never experienced that family closeness of the early years, and now in their early teens, they had joined the popular group of unsupervised, party-minded youngsters, experimenting with pot, attending keggers, wearing the latest sensual fads of the day.

Don lived more and more alone — bewildered, confused, wanting and needing parental guidance. He stated to his probation officer how much he missed being with his family in close companionship, but that he knew these times were gone forever. He spoke of endless nights alone, not knowing where his parents were or when they would return. He told of his sisters' activities and his concern for them. He expressed need for peer companionship, and his inability to make friends. He spoke of the act that resulted in his being before the court, and he wept.

Seated directly behind Don were his father and mother. Though they were distraught, they gave the impression that "this can't happen to us. We are good, moral people, well thought of in the community. We have a nice home, many friends. This is insulting, degrading that we should be in this court with a son who is charged with an illegal act. This is a bad dream. Surely it will go away!" They affected to look poised and controlled, yet were visibly shaken. Neither their tastefully dressed bodies nor their gracious, perfect manners could cover their embarrassment.

As I sat, observing the situation in the court room and mentally reviewing the background information supplied by the probation officer, the Word of the Lord moved in: "There is a way which seemeth right unto a man, but the end thereof are the ways of death ... the prudent man looketh well to his goings."

The court room was quiet. Out in the court yard, which could be seen through the drapery-drawn window, the flowers were ablaze with color. Beautiful, exotic birds mixed with the more common fowl to create a picture of the lofty and the common. Somehow, the court room scene mirrored this scene. The silence seemed loud and ominous. And then, the door to the judge's chambers opened.

"Please rise!"

The court clerk preceded the judge into the court room. She remained standing beside her recording equipment until the judge was seated. "Court is in session, you may be seated." Judgment had begun. The black robe of the judge added to the dignity of the court and seemed to be addressing itself to the seriousness of the moment.

The eyes of the judge rested on Don. He did not smile as he turned his eyes from Don to take a piercing sweep of the court room. His very air of authority demanded respect and a subservient attitude from all in his presence.

The attorney, appointed as guardian ad litem for Don, had taken his seat behind and to the left of the boy. His eyes shifted from the judge to Don. Perhaps he was thinking of comments Don had made to him in conference prior to the hearing. He was there to represent the best interests of Don and to see that the boy's constitutional rights were protected. If he fulfilled his responsibilities according to the Juvenile Code, his recommendation to the court would be what he felt would be in Don's best interests and might not be what Don or the probation officer would want. Time would tell.

The probation officer straightened his papers. He sat attentively. Don once more assumed his rigid position, but as his eyes met the judge's he dropped his head, working his hands together rapidly. He shifted his position several times and then seemed to slump with an exhausted, resigned expression. Behind him, his parents seated themselves cautiously, then nervously shifted. The father took the mother's hand as her tears began to flow; his jaw hardened, his determined look seemed to say, "I will not show my feelings." The court clerk turned on the recording equipment.

"This petition, filed by Mr. Langley, the probation officer," stated the judge, "comes on as a delinquency matter in the case of Donald Robert Aimes, who is alleged to be a delinquent in that on or about June

18, 1973, he did commit a delinquent act in that he did have in his possession ten lids of marijuana and does admit having smoked marijuana for the past three years. He also admits the use of other controlled substances, namely LSD and hashish, and to the sale of marijuana on at least one occasion. This sale was made to Shirley Porterfield on or about June 16, 1973, at Linder High School."

"Are you Donald Robert Aimes?" he asked of Don who nodded affirmatively.

"You will have to speak up; every word you say must be recorded. Raise your head. Speak loudly and directly into the microphone," directed the judge.

Don raised his head. "Yes," he stated firmly and into the microphone.

"Are you his parents?" asked the judge as he directed the question to father and mother.

"Yes," replied Mr. Aimes.

"Are the facts admitted?" the judge asked the guardian ad litem.

"He admits the facts, Your Honor. We can proceed informally," came the reply.

Turning to the probation officer, the judge asked for a background report, a review of the charges, and a recommendation.

"Your Honor," began the probation officer, "things haven't gone too well for Don lately. His parents tell me they were not aware he was involved in the drug scene. They also state they were not aware of some of Don's personal feelings. I am sure Don will share these with you. Mr. and Mrs. Aimes say they see Don's friends come to the home on occasion, but they really do not know his friends personally. Mr. Aimes indicates he feels a boy of seventeen should be able to choose his friends wisely. He also indicated they do not spend a great deal of time with their son because they feel a young man of Don's age certainly has interests which are his own, and he would resent parental interference.

"I asked his parents," continued Mr. Langley, "what kinds of activities the family enjoys as a unit. Mrs. Aimes told me they really have not been involved as a family since the children became teenagers. She also stated her husband's job and her responsibilities in the community take a great deal of time. Both Mr. and Mrs. Aimes expressed a concern as to whether Don would enjoy spending time with them, or whether he had outgrown them. I got the impression neither parent knows Don very well. They are shocked, however, with the most recent development and indicate they are at a loss to explain such behavior on the part of their son.

"Don admits to the use of the drugs," the probation officer continued. "He says that a majority of the young people at the high school use drugs, and this has become a way of life for the younger generation. He frankly admits he becomes very lonely, rarely sees his parents, and cannot recall the last conversation he had with them. He indicates they provide very well for him. They allow him to come and go as he pleases. They provide spending money and a car for him. They do not question his activities. He states he sold the marijuana, not because he needed the money, but because he wanted to make points with a young lady. He describes her as attractive and popular, and thought he might be able to spend some time with her. He frankly admits he was flattered that she would come to him, and that he felt pretty good that he could supply her with the marijuana.

"This is Don's second contact with the court, Your Honor. About four months ago he was arrested with a group of young people who were having a party which was unsupervised. There was a great deal of drinking going on. The police were called. The young people were scooped up and brought into the detention hall. Don was released to his parents on unofficial probation with specific rules. He and his parents had an opportunity to take a good long look at his way of life and to make some evaluations. But here he is again, on a much more serious charge.

"Mr. and Mrs. Aimes have been cooperative. They express a great deal of concern over what has happened, but I am not sure whether it is Don that causes their concern, or the upsetting situation in which he has placed the family. This is a family in which communication has broken down. Mother and father don't really know their son, the son does not know mother and father. I feel there is a great deal to build on, but at the moment the future looks bleak for Don unless definite changes are made. This young man needs supervision and guidance. He needs to establish a value system and some goals for his life. I am not sure his parents are going to be able to help him do this. I see them as needing direction for their own lives.

"My recommendation," stated the probation officer, "is that Don be placed outside the home for a period of time. This would accomplish two purposes. First, it would allow time for a diagnostic work-up on Don. This would provide insights into his behavior, his attitudes, and his interests, and would provide a basis for planning more appropriately for him. Second, this would provide time for Mr. and Mrs. Aimes to receive some needed counseling. I feel they need to gain a better understanding of their children and their own parenting role. There are two daughters who will be before the court soon if some changes are not made. Priorities which allow for family interaction and growth need to be established. Hopefully, Don can rejoin the family again, in time. But at the moment I do not feel this is advisable."

"Mr. Langley," said the judge, "you have hit upon some important facts. In the first place Don must understand that while he will be held responsible for his actions and will be dealt with accordingly, his parents share in this responsibility. It takes more than a biological act to become a parent! It takes more than material benefits to rear a child properly. Parenting is a full-time job! Now, what do you have to say for yourselves and your son, Mr. and Mrs. Aimes?"

The face of the judge was stern. His voice was demanding as he directed the question to the parents. All eyes were on the father as he began to speak.

"Your Honor, I don't understand. I just don't understand! We have felt we were good parents. We have provided well for our children. This boy has his own car. We don't ask anything of him. He comes and goes as he pleases and he has money in his pocket. He has so much more than I had when I was a boy! We have tried to be good to him. We are embarrassed, humiliated. We just don't understand why Don has done this to us. Very frankly, it will be hard to hold our heads up in the neighborhood after this. We just don't understand!"

"Mrs. Aimes, do you have any comment to make?" asked the judge.

"No. My husband has said it all. I just want to add — I think I have been a good mother to Don — to all my children." She sobbingly lowered her head.

"What do you have to say, Don?" asked the judge. "Speak up! Tell me what is on your mind. This is a serious violation. Not only have you broken the law, but you have been instrumental in assisting someone else to do so. I want to know where you are getting this stuff and why you made such a decision."

"Mr. Langley is right in everything he said. I know what I have done is wrong. Drugs are just there and easy to get. It sort of makes you forget and unwind. You don't feel so uptight about things. I told the officers where I bought it. I am sorry I have hurt my parents — I didn't think it would hurt them that much. I guess I really didn't think. As Mr. Langley said, I do need some help. Things have been sort of mixed up lately. I know that is no excuse, but they really have been. I have been worried about my sisters and about my parents. I have been doing a lot of thinking since I have been in the cell. I wish we could all go back . . ." his voice broke. The judge did not pressure.

"I am glad to hear you are not making excuses, Don. This court will hold you accountable for your actions and views this as a very serious violation. You are destroying yourself, and you are helping to destroy others. This I will not tolerate." Turning to the guardian, Judge Robinson asked, "What is your recommendation?"

"Your Honor," replied the attorney, "I agree with the recommendation of the probation officer. I feel Don has a great deal of strength. I believe he knows right from wrong. He stated to me he would like to go home, but he knows he needs help. I agree with the probation officer — I do not feel his parents are able, at this time, to provide that help. Although we don't have too much time in the juvenile system to work with this family, I feel they are worth every effort we can expend in this direction. Don has an uncle out of state who is very interested in him. Mr. Langley has spoken with this gentleman by telephone. The uncle understands the problem and will do everything he can to assist. He is willing to have Don undergo a psychiatric or psychological evaluation, and to make this report available to the court. I believe this home would meet the present need."

The crucial moment of decision had come. The judge must now exercise the authority vested in him and pass judgment on the actions of the young man. He must do so within the framework of the law based on the evidence as presented. He must uphold the law, despite his own personal feelings. The court room was hushed as all present intently waited for the words of the judge. Momentarily looking down at the pad upon which he had written some notes, the judge raised his head and for a brief moment his eyes swept the court room and then rested on Don.

"After hearing the facts of the case and listening carefully to the testimony presented, I am ready to make my decision. But before I do so, I have a few things I would like to say to you, Mr. and Mrs. Aimes." The judge's voice was forceful and strong as he prepared to pass the judgment of the court. His whole being seemed to overwhelm the room, and the power and authority of the office was felt in his tone of voice.

"I am amazed at what I have heard," began the judge. "But, in reviewing the file, I am more amazed when I think of how things were with you as a family a few years ago. I sense no real love, at least not an awareness of what love really means, in anything you have said. You are embarrassed — you are humiliated — you cannot hold your head up in your neighborhood! You are thinking only of yourselves! Your concern is measured in terms of material benefits, inconvenience to yourselves, and your own reputation! Not once have you thought of your son's welfare, his needs, his feelings! You had better take a good look at what you are doing not only to your children but to yourselves. Your value system is all wrong! Face your responsibility here, and do something about it. Then come back and tell me you are the parents of this young man.

"Now, Don, before you feel too comfortable, I have some things to say to you. You have been in trouble before. You were given an opportunity to square yourself away. You did not. I am sure you were aware of the consequences if you came here again. You went your own way. You did as you pleased, disregarding the law and the penalty for breaking the law. You are accountable and without excuse. While it is true you received no help from your parents, you are not a baby. You knew what you were doing when you made the decisions you did."

Don seemed to wilt before the judge. He seemed to realize the power vested in the court. He seemed visibly shaken by the words just spoken.

"Donald," said the judge, "I am going to place you on a suspended commitment to the Department of Institutions. I am also going to send you to your uncle under strict rules of probation. You are to reside with your uncle, undergo a psychiatric evaluation, and follow every rule. If you don't get your head screwed on straight, you are going to meet another judge someday who will not give you another chance! Don't blow it.

"Mr. and Mrs. Aimes, get yourself into some counseling. I am sure Mr. Langley will assist you, and advise you where you can get this help. I hope you have learned something here today. Your son needs you. Your two daughters need you. They are important. I hope you realize that. I can only wish you the very best as I solemnly warn you."

As everyone stood quietly, the judge left the court room.

Judgment had been passed. Don seemed relieved. Mr. and Mrs. Aimes went immediately to their son. There were tearful embraces. The probation officer joined them to give final directives. The court clerk turned off the recording equipment. She and the attorney left the room.

As I left the court room, Don's father spoke to him: "It won't be for long, son. We will all get together — really together, again, very soon."

Perhaps the judge really did get through, after all!

Chapter 5

The juvenile court judge often points out that whatever occupies the thoughts directs the life: "Judging is my life," he states. "It invades every phase of my life, twenty-four hours a day. You are no different. If drugs, or stealing, or burglary, or armed robbery, or prostitution is your life, it will interfere with your every thought, twenty-four hours a day. Your heart is in your thoughts!"

To the child who rationalizes his involvement in unlawful activities, the juvenile court judge has choice words of wisdom for him to ponder. "You are being irresponsible! Until you realize your own responsibility for your actions, you will never change. Must I lock you up before you can become productive? Are you so weak you can't make up your own mind? Do you mean to tell me you do everything your friends do? I don't buy that. You wanted to go along. You made the decision. Until you grow up and learn to say no, you will take the consequences. Where are your friends now? I don't see them sitting here! If you share everything with them, why don't they do the same for you? Do you have an answer for that? Well, you had better find one, or you will be in trouble the rest of your life!"

To the parents who rationalize, "he got in with the wrong kind of people," the judge reminds them: "Someone is saying that about your child too — the wrong kind of people!"

Lenny's home life was troubled, but his choices were his own.

LENNY ...

"Without Me, you can do nothing."

On this cold, rainy day, the court room was chilled by the slouching figure of Lenny, who was waiting in his assigned seat for the judge to enter the room. His face showed anger, hostility, contempt. The anxious, drawn expression on his mother's face only added to the chill of despair and hopelessness.

Lenny was a tall, thin boy of fourteen. His record revealed he was from a large family of seven boys and one girl. According to information received from Mrs. Carter, Lenny's mother, the father was an alcoholic. Her husband, when home, could be found "sleeping it off on the davenport," or beating her or one of the children. She frankly admitted there was no communication between her husband and herself, or between him and the children. He insisted that the family "do it my way," never giving an explanation or reason. When his demands were not met, he immediately resorted to the bottle. He worked hard, but there was little money with which the needs of the family could be met. As a result, it was necessary for Mrs. Carter to seek employment outside the home. Following a full day at her secretarial duties, Mrs. Carter spent long evenings working about her home in an effort to keep things as comfortable as possible for the children. She frequently spoke of the hours spent in washing, ironing, canning, and baking.

Mrs. Carter seemed to be a very kind, gentle person. But she was over-protective of her children. By her own admission she and her husband had no common ground regarding child rearing practices. The children appeared to dislike their father intensely. They deliberately disobeyed him, knowing their mother would come to their defense. They excused their disobedience, saying, "he doesn't know what he is doing any way ... it always has to be his way ... he never gives a reason ...." They encouraged their mother to leave their father, and when she did not oblige them, they seemed to delight in increasing her anxiety by the most inappropriate behavior. The older boys were fighters, eventually becoming involved in the use of drugs and in other illegal acts. In time, the younger children followed in their footsteps, refusing to go to school, disobeying, attempting to break up the home, and generally exhibiting incorrigible behavior. Through all of this Mrs. Carter cooperated with the authorities in the community and in the school in an effort to provide educational opportunities for the children and to keep them out of trouble.

Lenny had a record of being a chronic truant. As a result, he was receiving failing marks. When he was in school, his behavior was appropriate, but his attendance had become of grave concern to the school authorities. Many conferences had been held with the mother in an attempt to establish an adequate attendance pattern for her son. Nothing had worked. This was the basis for the court hearing, but not the charge as outlined in the delinquency petition.

The situation which brought Lenny before the court had actually begun in my office a few days prior to the hearing. Lenny had been referred to me on a suspension from his principal for excessive truancy. Because of the failure of past efforts, and because of the State Compulsory Attendance Law, this was a crucial situation. Something had to be done.

Mrs. Carter had brought him to my office before going to work. It was early. Half asleep, Lenny appeared angry at having to report to me. As Mrs. Carter and I reviewed the past unsuccessful efforts to get Lenny to attend school, Lenny sat scowling, answering his mother in a sassy manner, if at all. Finally, in desperation, Mrs. Carter said, "Please take him to the Hall. I cannot manage him. He needs help and I can't give it to him. He won't mind and he will eventually destroy himself. I have to go to work, but I would appreciate it if you would do this for me — and for Lenny." She had tears in her eyes; her voice was barely a whisper. She turned and left the office.

Lenny got to his feet. I had other scheduled appointments, so I knew I would not be able to take Lenny to the Hall. Because I felt he would run from me, I made a rapid decision. I would have him be seated, and then in some way, without his knowledge, I would call for assistance from the juvenile officers. With this thought in mind, I directed Lenny to take a seat near the front of the office. I was walking behind him when I heard one of the district school principals yell "Watch out! He has a knife!"

Lenny was turning toward me, the steel blade of the knife glistening. He had it opened and his hand was raised to strike when the principal and a co-worker grabbed his arm, thrusting it back. Lenny wrestled with them. To avoid hurting him they requested assistance from another staff member who had heard the commotion and had come in from the hall. The three men were careful not to hurt Lenny, which was a struggle for them since he was squirming, kicking, and biting.

I stood to the side, unable to comprehend fully what had taken place. Regaining perspective, I directed the secretary to call the juvenile authorities. When the officer arrived, Lenny was still fighting, his conduct indicating to the officer that he would perhaps require more direct treatment than the school officials had meted out. The officer, using one hand, took hold of Lenny and said, "Now, if you are going to act like a man, you will be treated like one."

Lenny's response was to exert greater effort to get away and to lash out the most uncomplimentary adjectives imaginable in describing the school staff and the officer. With this outburst, he was handcuffed and placed in a chair, his hands behind the back of the chair.

While the officer was taking the report from those of us in the room, Lenny began working his cuffed hands down under his feet. In some way he had managed to work his hands under the chair and was now bringing them under his feet. The officer reached him just as his hands came up and he was swinging at the man. For his effort, Lenny was rewarded by having his hands cuffed to his belt. The officer then picked him up by the back of his belt and walked out with him kicking, screaming, and threatening to "get even" with all of us.

After regaining some degree of composure, I called Lenny's mother. She was shocked! Her concern was for those of us who had been involved. She seemed relieved that Lenny was now in custody, that he did not run, and that perhaps she would now receive the assistance she needed.

Seated in the court room, waiting for the judge to enter, I thought of her distress. While she no doubt contributed to her own problems, I could not help but think of the heartache she had suffered. Sin is so costly! As I exchanged glances with Mrs. Carter, she smiled — a sad little smile, but even that revealed her courage, hope, and a longing for better days ahead.

Often as I had spoken with Mrs. Carter, she had expressed a personal faith and belief that the Lord would somehow work things out for her and the children. She did not attend church, and gave as her excuse her busy schedule. Despite her permissive ways with her children, she appeared to have at the core of her very existence the well-being of the children. But, with all of her problems, she reflected a strength unknown to many. She expectantly looked ahead — without adequate direction, true, but with an indescribable hope! She refused to succumb to her problems!

Following Lenny's arrest, I had spoken with him for about two hours one evening. He had settled down, but firmly stated he would have used the knife. I did not believe him. I felt his purpose was to delay what he knew was inevitable — being taken to the juvenile hall. I also felt he was a stubborn, rebellious child who would never be able to admit, at least for a time, that he had made a serious mistake. That evening I shared with Lenny the reason I felt his plan to use the knife was not carried out: the Lord protects His own in the midst of danger. In this very experience, I was an example of His promise: "For he shall give his angels charge over thee, to keep thee in all thy ways." Lenny laughed at this. He discussed his mother's professed faith, but countered that were her faith so real things would be different at home. He used the home situation as an excuse for his actions. He blamed his father for what he termed unreasonable treatment, and his mother for lenient, permissive treatment of the children. He frankly admitted using the situation for personal gain. I challenged him with the responsibility of being a productive member of the family, rather than one so weak as to blame others. If Lenny felt a need for the Lord in his life, he surely would not acknowledge it. He seemed to be a bitter, vindictive youngster! I knew he would be in far more serious trouble if his attitudes were unchanged.

Now he was charged with attempted assault with a deadly weapon! This could mean confinement in the Department of Institutions. Was this the answer? What was my responsibility to this boy and to his family?

"Please rise!"

The voice of the clerk of the court called each of us to our feet as the juvenile court judge entered the room. "You may be seated. Court is now in session."

Judge Benson brought dignity to his court. He demanded the attention and respect of all in attendance. As his piercing eyes met Lenny's and his serious expression blended with the already tense atmosphere, Lenny straightened himself in his seat; his angry look slowly disappeared; and he faced the judge with an expression of submission to the authority of the court — an attitude foreign to those of us who had previously worked with him. Observing him now, it was evident there would be no contest. In fact, Lenny appeared almost relieved!

"Young man," Judge Benson addressed Lenny, "I have read your file. You are charged with attempted assault with a deadly weapon. Your past history leaves no doubt that you are an incorrigible, delinquent child. You have been disobedient in the home. You have refused to attend school. You have flaunted the laws in the face of those in authority over you. And now you face the court, charged with one of the most stupid, but one of the most dangerous acts you could commit. I don't know whether you realize what the consequences of your act could have been, but let's get something straight now. I view this as a very serious violation of the law and will deal with it accordingly. Now, I want you to tell me why you did it. And I want the truth — no beating around the bush, straight facts."

There was a moment's silence. Lenny seemed so alone. As though the weight of guilt had settled down on his shoulders, he slumped momentarily, then straightened himself to full sitting height and began. "I did it because I was mad. I did not want to be put in jail."

"Don't you think you had it coming?" asked the judge.

"Yeah," replied Lenny, "but I didn't want to come. I thought I could run. I don't like school. I don't like home. My folks don't get along. It is a drag."

"Whose fault is that?" asked the judge.

"Probably all of ours. But I get tired of a bunch of creeps telling me what to do, where to go, and what I can say," Lenny responded.

"What is that supposed to mean, young man? Don't you think your parents have a right to tell you what to do, and don't you think the school authorities have the right to expect you to obey the law and be in school?" queried the judge.

"I guess so," said Lenny, "but there is a lot more to it than that."

"Well, then, suppose you tell me. But one thing I want to know — did you plan to use the knife?" asked the judge.

"Yes," Lenny's reply was definite.

There was a pause — a loud pause in the court. Disbelief flooded the mother's face. The probation officer looked startled as though he were thinking, "Well, that does it; it is all over now...." I felt weak.

I could not help but think that I was among the "bunch of creeps" Lenny referred to. I waited, praying that when my time came to speak, I would have the directive I needed to speak with some semblance of wisdom and understanding regarding this child's need.

"Well, Lenny, you leave me no choice," said Judge Benson. "By your own admission, the intent of your actions is clear. I would like to hear from the probation officer regarding his investigation and recommendation."

Mr. Schwartz, a very capable probation officer, always presented his investigations in a complete, concise manner. He began to speak.

"Your Honor, in order to present to the court a most accurate picture of the total situation, I would like to request the court hear from the mother following my report. This is my first contact with Lenny. I have made every effort to establish within my own mind an honest, adequate appraisal of the situation and to assess Lenny's needs in the light of established facts. I trust his best interests are in proper perspective as I present my findings to the court. This is a family in which there is no communication between father and mother, the mother, consequently, assuming the responsible role. Father bows out, resorting to the bottle or abusive behavior toward his wife and children. He is either prohibited by his wife's actions or through a weakness of his own from taking the responsibility he should take in the home. As a result, the children are suffering. I do not doubt the sincerity of the mother in her efforts to compensate for her husband's inadequacies, but the result is that these children, including Lenny, are experiencing a destructive psychological deprivation. As a result we have a youngster before the court who has developed a defiant, hostile attitude toward all authority and control, and who is willing, or was willing, to get his way by force and by placing another life in danger. Yes, he told me he intended to use the knife. I believe him. If it please the court, I would defer making my recommendation to the court until the mother is heard from."

The judge turned to the mother. "Your Honor," tears came to Mrs. Carter's eyes as she began. "I do blame myself. Mr. Schwartz is right. I think Lenny is a good boy. I do love him. I am just happy he did not do what he tried to do, and that he is safe here in court. I am willing to do whatever the court orders, but I do want help — for Lenny and for my family. I know we need it. Things are really mixed up. I don't know what the outcome will be. I know he has to be responsible for what he has done. I would like to have him home, but I don't know whether the court will let me do that. And, I really don't know what is best for Lenny."

"Mrs. Carter," Judge Benson stated, "You see before you a situation which is the direct result of a divided household. By that I mean a father and a mother not working together, not understanding what the other is attempting to do, not willing to communicate, going in opposite directions and pulling their children with them. All behavior is learned, and here is a classic example of a boy who has had no security, no consistency, no guidance, no guidelines, no direction in his life because of the selfishness of two adults determined to have their own way. However, that does not permit me to hold this young man any less responsible for what he has done. He is not a baby. He should be able to put two and two together and come up with four. I will not tolerate excuses on his part, although I will frankly state I feel you share in the blame. But, because he committed the act, it is he I must deal with. That is one of the limitations of the juvenile system. It is unfortunate the parent cannot be charged with the child." The mother dropped her eyes under the pressure of the comments from the court. The judge turned to the probation officer.

"What is your recommendation?"

"Your Honor, I have no choice but to recommend commitment to the Department of Institutions. I feel Lenny needs some professional help he cannot receive in any other placement. I think he needs to be out of the community for a time."

Lenny did not flinch at the recommendation. Neither did his mother. I suppose I was the one who felt the pressure the most at the moment. If, indeed, the situation had been brought about through circumstances as presented to the court, surely there was another way. Should not this youngster have an opportunity — some place other than the Institution? I thought of a comment Lenny made when he and I conferenced. "My grandparents live across the state. I used to live near them. I like them." Perhaps this was a resource.

"Your Honor," I interrupted, "may I speak?"

"I was going to get to you," said the judge. "What do you have to say about this?"

"I have known Lenny for almost a year — a very hectic relationship, true, but this time has given me an opportunity to get to know the family to a degree, and to have the opportunity to conference with Lenny on several occasions. On this particular occasion, which subsequently resulted in Lenny's arrest, it is true I was going to have him placed in detention for his failure to attend school. This action, I felt, was necessary because there was no other resource than to appeal to the court for assistance. I do not believe he would have used the knife. I may be wrong. But I feel he was as desperate as I. He lashed out at his level of understanding, just as he felt I was lashing out at him with my anticipated action. In his frame of mind, he had no other recourse, just as I had no other. I have since had the opportunity to speak at length with him. We talked seriously about his responsibilities despite his home life, his future, and the fact that his future would be determined by the direction he chooses now regarding home, school, and the community. I agree with Mr. Schwartz — he needs a change of environment, one in which he can receive help, direction, and guidance. But I would like to recommend an alternative to the Institution. Lenny has grandparents of whom he is very fond. I would respectfully request of the court that he be allowed to live with them for a time. Perhaps in that way he can put things in proper perspective in relation to his home and his responsibilities here."

I shrank inwardly under the gaze of the judge. But I held outwardly firm in my exchange of stares with him. After what seemed several minutes, the judge spoke. "Do you honestly think that would work?"

"No," I replied, "not without imposing an added dimension of counseling, supervision, and probation rules regarding activities, curfew, and so on. A change of environment just for its own sake will not necessarily work, but I think a change of environment with positive reinforcement would be most beneficial."

"How about this as an alternative placement?" the judge asked of the probation officer.

"Your Honor, this placement is available, and I have no objection, if the court so orders. But I agree there must be supplementary forces which would allow for an environment in which this boy could receive the psychological support he seems so desperately to need."

Directing his question to the mother, the judge inquired, "Do you have any objections to such a placement?"

"No," she faintly replied. It was evident she was so near tears and emotional exhaustion she dare not speak up for fear of losing control. The court addressed Lenny. "How do you feel about this?"

"I would like that," Lenny replied without hesitation, and for the first time a slight smile was visible on his face.

"Very well," stated the judge. "I will make such an order. I want Lenny held here until transportation can be arranged for him. I want it made very plain that you are to abide by rules of probation as imposed by this court. Mr. Schwartz, I want you to write out his rules of probation, and I want him supervised by the court in his grandparents' home town. And, young man, if you come before me again, there will be no second chance. You are being separated from all things you have said are a hindrance to your adjustment. But you are taking with you one most important thing — your own personal responsibility and accountability to those in charge of you and to those in authority over you. What you do with this opportunity is up to you. And while he is gone, I hope, Mr. Schwartz, you will arrange for some counseling assistance for the family so that in time they can all be reunited. But, from my point of view, there will of necessity have to be many changes before we can see positive results."

The judge rose. Everyone in the court stood to attention as he left the room.

I sat for a moment wondering whether this decision really was in Lenny's best interest. I was not convinced he was not already damaged so badly that he would not be able to abide by rules of probation.

Lenny turned toward his mother. Going to him and placing her arms around him, she expressed her joy in the disposition of the court, at the same time pointing out to Lenny his need to obediently follow the rules of probation. Lenny stood motionless. Whether he was affected by his mother's plea was not evident. He walked out of the court room with the probation officer without offering his mother any assurance that things would be better. She left, after thanking each of us for our help and stating her appreciation and hope that Lenny would soon be reunited with the family, assuring us that there would be extended effort on her part and on the part of her husband to solidify their own relationship and work out the problems in the home.

I lingered a moment, thinking of the genuine effort Mrs. Carter was making — in her own strength — and how futile it really was! Jesus said, "Without Me, you can do nothing."

Lenny went to live with his grandparents. He completed the eighth grade before he returned to his home at the beginning of the fall term. He did very well while living with his grandparents. However, because of their age and the distance needed to travel, Lenny did not receive counseling assistance. Living on the farm, in a small community, was good for Lenny. He gained weight, made good grades, and seemed more content when he returned to his family with permission of his probation officer.

Coming home, where conditions had not changed, and joining his old companions proved too much for Lenny. Within months he had committed several burglaries and was in court once again. On this occasion he was committed to the Department of Institutions. In Lenny's words, it was here he learned his first "big lesson in manipulation." Following his stay in the diagnostic center, he was placed in a forestry camp. There, he says, he soon learned how extra privileges were earned. He determined to do his best, but his goal was not improvement; he merely wanted to get out. He achieved his objective and was released by the end of the school year, to return to his home.

"Things were no different," states Lenny. He entered high school, but was soon in trouble over the length of his hair, smoking, and cutting classes. Lenny cites an example of getting in trouble with his algebra teacher. He is a whiz at math, but he wanted, at that time, to do it his way. He explained that he came up "with the right answers, but she insisted I do it her way. I refused." So he walked out of class. He lasted in school two weeks.

Lenny got himself mixed up with drugs. "I tried speed, LSD, and a lot of things without labels. Fortunate they weren't bad, that is, I didn't kill myself. I liked going on trips ... never had any bad trips ... but I enjoyed the hallucinogenic drugs." When asked what attraction drugs really had for him, he explained "drugs were controversial. I tried them to defy the system. It was something like an open door, or a look at a movie. My experience was my own, not like any one else's. I had what I called successful experiences, but not beneficial ... I see that now. I was revoked, and sent back to the Institution by my parole counselor because I could not adjust."

Lenny was once again assigned to a forestry camp, different from the first, but where he was required to do manual labor and earn points which led to privileges. "My second lesson in manipulation, and I did such a good job I was out in four months. I took orders long enough to be placed in a position where I could give them, and it turned out well for me ... or so I thought ... I went home."

"At that time," Lenny explained, "I entered school again, the second try at tenth grade. It didn't work. I left home. I slept in the back of cars, was using drugs extensively. I had no food, and I was drinking."

He was revoked again and was returned to the Department of Institutions for the third time and assigned, once again, to a forestry program. By this time, Lenny was seventeen.

Before he was revoked he came to see me. He was dirty and smelly and he looked emaciated. He wanted help. He had a friend with him who looked as bad as he did. I spoke very frankly with Lenny at that time about his need of the Lord. I made an offer to him. I told him I would rent an apartment for him and supply it with food for one month if he would agree to attend church services in the church of my choice on Sundays and also agree not to have pot parties in the apartment. This offer seemed to appeal to him and he began to ask questions. "What about my hair?" It was long, stringy and dirty!

"All I ask," I replied, "is that you wash it. You may sit where you like in church. You do not need to acknowledge knowing me. I only ask that you attend one month. At the end of that month there are no obligations. You may do as you please. During that time, I will not see you, except at church, unless you want to see me. But I will expect you to keep your word, if you agree to this arrangement. I will purchase the food for you. I will not give you money, because I do not feel you would spend it properly. I don't want you to give me your answer now. Think about it, and let me know."

Lenny sat for a long time pondering the offer. Finally he spoke. "If I agree, you mean all I will have to do is go to church on Sunday, have the food I need and an apartment for a month?"

"That is right," was my reply.

"I find that hard to believe," Lenny said. "That wouldn't be hard to do."

"Then why don't you do it?" I asked.

At that point Lenny's friend cautioned him. "Hey, man, this is a trick. You better think about it."

"Yeah, I guess so ... but I don't think it is a trick. I'll think about it and I'll come back and let you know." He rose to go. "I'll let you know," he promised. Lenny left. He did not return. He called a few days later to say he had "thought about it" but he "guessed not."

A few days later he was revoked for burglary. Lenny had made another decision. He had no food, he felt a need for drugs, so he burglarized and was caught. He was sent to yet another forestry camp, where he was placed on a work–release program three days before his eighteenth birthday and went to work for the Department of Natural Resources, working on a rock crusher. Things went well for six months. Then he was changed to a job nearer home and he moved home, commuting to his work each day. At the same time, he picked up with the old friends and the night life. His drive to the job required him to drive over mountain roads. One morning, according to Lenny, he was on his way to work and awoke with two wheels on the road. He made a choice. He quit his job and once again started bumming around. He was near nineteen by that time.

"I took a course in Moving and Packing at the vocational school, but I bombed out of that. My grandfather had left some money to each of us kids when he died. I took that money and entered community college, but I still hung on to my old friends. So I withdrew, earning no credits, my money gone. I then began working out of the Labor Union Hall. I had some good jobs, earned some good money; things were looking up. I got married one day after my twenty-first birthday. I was doing fine until I was injured on the job. I did get a settlement, but I have ten percent partial permanent disability. After I left camp the third time, I quit drinking, quit the drugs, and really began to think things through."

"What conclusions have you come to, Lenny?" I asked. "I can see it now," he began. "I know I need an education. I have enrolled once again in the community college and I am going to major in math. I want to teach math some day. About home — we never did sit down and talk things over."

Lenny expresses no bitterness about his incarceration at the juvenile level. He feels he learned lessons he could not have learned elsewhere. But he is sure of one thing — he does not want to experience incarceration at the adult level. He is determined that he will live in such a way as to prevent this possibility. He has not settled things with the Lord, but as he puts it, "I know I have to deal with that . . . some day."

Let's hope he does not wait too long. He has heard. The responsibility is his.

Part Two

The Dependent Child

Chapter 6

Dependency is defined differently in different states. A general definition of a dependent is a child against whom a crime has been committed. The dependent child shall mean any child under a specified age who comes to the attention of the court through no fault of his own. He is the victim of conditions which prevail within his environment and over which he has no control. Dependent children then are the victims of crime.

Dependent children are brought to the court from a variety of circumstances. They include the neglected, the abandoned, the runaway, and the incorrigible.

State laws vary in defining neglect. Generally speaking, a child is considered neglected if under a certain age he is denied the physical necessities of life, appropriate medical care, and educational opportunities. The neglected child makes up a large segment of dependent children.

Neglect takes many forms. A filthy home may be sufficient cause for charging neglect. Inadequate supervision is considered to be a form of neglect in some states, though children vary in this need. The age of the child is often the criterion used to establish his ability to supervise himself. Immoral or unlawful conduct on the part of the parents may result in a charge of neglect. Such a child is being exposed to a pattern of life that is not in his best interest. Police raids on homes where excessive partying or drug possession or use is found may result in referral of children. These youngsters are usually taken to the court for shelter care, for their presence in such homes indicates they are improperly supervised. Juveniles found to be frequenting questionable places of business are also brought to the attention of the court.

Abandoned children are considered neglected in many states. An abandoned child is one whose parent has left him with someone for a designated length of time, but fails to return within a reasonable time thereafter. Or, an abandoned child may be one whose parents have failed to visit for an inexcusable length of time — perhaps the child in foster or group care. An abandoned child may also be one whose parent has not supported him for a long period of time. Children of divorced parents are sometimes said to be abandoned by the father for failure to support. It may be that the child has no home in which he can live. This may be of a temporary nature due to illness or death in the family, or of a more permanent form. With no proper guardian and without subsistence, he must rely on the court to take action on his behalf.

Under some state statutes runaways are considered dependent. Although a child does his own running, it is believed that a running child is a dependent child because he is running from something or someone in his environment. The run takes place when he feels he can no longer cope. The runaway frequently becomes involved in delinquencies.

Truants are classified as dependents in many states. This is difficult to understand. Most often parents are supportive in asking the child to attend school regularly. In fact, many parents go so far as to take the child to school each day. He may enter the building, but he leaves through another door. Perhaps truants are "school runaways!" It may be that they cannot cope with school. Their manner of running is simply labeled truancy. Court action is often necessary to break the habit.

The incorrigible child, or status offender, is also classified as dependent. This is the child who is out of control in the home, who refuses to obey the rules of the home. He is defined by the court as a dependent-incorrigible. These rebellious children often become delinquent.

Status offenders are of grave concern to the federal government. States have been placed on notice to arrange for more satisfactory housing for them. Institutionalization, it is felt, is not the answer, nor is it legal under the statutes. Specified federal funds will be withheld from states not meeting this demand. Some states have already begun work on this. Washington State's governor recently signed a bill into law prohibiting the institutionalization of such children.

Who refers the dependent child to the court? Parents, in the case of incorrigible children, are frequently the source of referrals. Referrals come from well-meaning neighbors and often from relatives. Children may refer themselves in some instances.

Cases involving crimes against children are more difficult to work with than cases involving children who are alleged to be delinquent. Needed cooperation is very difficult to obtain from the adult offender, since the court action, though based solely on attempting to meet the needs of the child, may carry prosecution for the adult who admits the facts. Cooperation is equated with the admission of guilt. In addition, law enforcement personnel, when called to investigate such cases, have a difficult time determining whether dependency exists. Social agencies called in to assist are equally frustrated. The question soon arises as to whose standards are being imposed. Not all homes function at the same level.

Legal proof of dependency is another matter. Statutes protect the rights of the biological parent as well as the child. Legal counsel is available for all such parents. Facts must be proved beyond a shadow of a doubt, requiring careful observation and investigation. The position of the juvenile court is never to separate a child from his family if the family can provide for him. It must be proved that the home is detrimental to the child.

Parents and children involved in the adjudication of dependency hearings are threatened, the threat coming not only from the court, but from society as a whole. When value systems are compared, when the opinions of others are imposed, when the most personal areas of life are exposed to public view, feeling runs high. Parents sometimes express the feeling of being an outcast. Children seem to feel a bit different from other children. The scars left are sometimes deep.

Come with me into the court and you will understand as you sit through the hearing of Wendi. You will witness the depths of the scars as you share her story from early childhood to the present.

WENDI ...

"The Lord is not through with me yet."

As Wendi and her probation officer entered the court room, Wendi was giggling in her own infectious way! She was a beautiful fifteen year old. Standing straight and tall, her long hair neatly combed, her slender figure poised, and her eyes expectantly challenging, Wendi exuded spring. She was vibrant! When she entered a room, she caught everyone's attention by her refreshing, outgoing manner, as though she were holding out arms of welcome to the world, saying, "Here I am. I want everything you have to offer, and if there should by chance be more adversity for me, you will not get me down ... I am ready!" Wendi had a way of making one forget his own problems in the confidence and hope she was able to communicate.

"Sit here, Wendi," her probation officer held the chair for her.

"Oh, do I get to have the honored seat?"

"You surely do," replied Mrs. Brown, "right in front of His Honor!"

"Hey, that's great! I'll have him all to myself. I think Judge Simms is the greatest! He is really nice to the kids." Wendi was referring to the fact that the judge always spoke with the children in the dining room when he was at the juvenile court. She had become acquainted with him in the short time she had been in the Hall. She felt about him as she seemed to feel about everyone — she enjoyed the time she was allowed to have with him and genuinely appreciated his attention.

Mrs. Brown pushed Wendi's chair forward. Instantly, Wendi pushed it back and rose to her feet. She threw her arms around her probation officer, hugged her tightly, and gave her a kiss on the cheek.

"Thank you, Mrs. Brown, I love you. You have been so good to me. You will come to see me, won't you?"

"Of course, Dear," Mrs. Brown's voice was choked. "You sit down now and look pretty for His Honor. We don't want him to see us at anything but our best, do we?"

"No, he won't," promised Wendi, "but I just wanted you to know." She giggled again, then with her face radiantly relaxed, she sat for a brief moment. Then, as though she instantly returned to reality, she quickly rose from her chair, came over to me and said, "Thank you for everything!" Leaning down, she kissed me on the cheek and whispered in my ear, "I love you! Please don't forget me. Come to see me." Then as quickly as she had approached me, she was back in her chair, smiling, appearing as though she did not have a care in the world. But in that one brief moment when she said "please don't forget me," I heard the cry of this lonely little girl's heart and knew that while the world would see the smiles, the heartache and the scars from deep, deep hurts would always remain. Wendi's courage was a rebuke to me.

To the casual observer this court room scene would have appeared joyful. At long last, Wendi was to be placed in a living situation which would be permanent until she reached her eighteenth birthday. She would have a home — a place to live where she would not fear removal on a moment's notice, a place where she would have the opportunity to grow, to mature socially and emotionally, to work toward her goals. Certainly we could all rejoice, but there was more to it than that! And this is what concerned me. Each of us in the court room was involved in the life of this young girl, and each of us must make a decision as to what role we would play.

Wendi had been at the Hall for several weeks. I had become well acquainted with her. Initially attracted to her by her winning ways, my feeling for her had grown much deeper than thinking of her as a sweet little girl who had been fun to know. It had been my privilege to sit and chat with her for long periods of time. She had shared some of the deep, deep feelings which were as real as the genuine smile she had for all. Waiting for the judge to enter the court room, I thought of these things.

Wendi had come to the attention of the court at the death of her mother when she was twelve years old. Knowing Wendi as I did, I felt she fought the idea of being a dependent. She wanted so to belong! She loved and wanted love. She dreamt of sharing as a member of a family. She longed for the security of being a part of a family. She did not want just a placement. She wanted a home!

As a child Wendi had experienced much deprivation. Her mother was an alcoholic. She never knew her real father, but she had known five stepfathers.

"Mother drank a lot, and loved a lot," said Wendi. "As a person, she had serious problems, one of them being men. She was always looking for something, wanting independence, but so dependent...."

Wendi, her brother, and her mother and whoever happened to be her current stepfather, moved around a great deal, living in one place or another until she, her brother, and mother would be left alone. Because of her own dependencies, her mother would remarry, and the vicious circle would begin all over. Wendi characterized her mother as "warm and outgoing, with a lot of love for my brother and me. She always saw to it that we had food, and she loved us a lot."

When Wendi was twelve, she was living above an Eighty-eight Cent store in a hotel room with her mother and current stepfather. Her brother had quit school and at seventeen had entered the service. Wendi's mother had had cancer and was now in the hospital with a recurrence. "While she was in the hospital," said Wendi, "I spent a lot of time with the lady in the store downstairs. The neighbors were good to me too. They helped me with the food and the house. I remember it was December 30. I had been to see my mother at the hospital ... you know, she was only thirty-eight, and she had cancer again. When I left the hospital, I knew she was dying. I spent a long time in the park, just thinking. When I went home, my stepfather had received a call telling him she was dead. He couldn't tell me. The lady in the store told me. I remember sitting on the counter and she tried to tell me. I put my arm around her and told her I knew my mother was dead. My brother came home from the service and we had the funeral, and then nobody knew what to do with me. My stepfather could not keep me. They asked me where I wanted to live. Once before, we had lived in this city and we had some nice neighbors. They were older than my mother, but they had been real nice to me. I decided I wanted to live with them, and I did."

A second chapter opened in Wendi's life. She was made a temporary ward of the court and moved to the home of her friends. She did not see her stepfather again. She explains this for him by saying "we hardly knew one another." Her foster parents were much older and once again Wendi was sort of on her own. She lost contact with her brother. The boy next door became her companion. He was an only child. His parents were younger than her foster parents, and their interests were more attuned to the needs of children, so Wendi clung to this new relationship. She and her new-found companion shared many interests and she felt very close to this family.

Wendi began to grow up. She was in the eighth grade. She describes it this way: "I guess I had adjustment problems. My foster parents felt they could not care for me any longer, and so with the permission of the court they sent me out of state to live with their older daughter, her husband and their three children. That was impossible! I was just a maid! Never went out, always babysitting, doing the ironing and housework. There was no communication. Under the pretense of a vacation, they brought me back. You can imagine how terrible I felt when I was met at the depot by two big police officers and they brought me to the Hall. I felt like it was the end of the world! I had no idea this was the plan. That really hurt, because I had tried. I needed a mother and I wanted a mother, but I could find no one who would even act like a mother."

On this occasion, Wendi was returned to the Hall and a court hearing followed. She remained a short time at the Hall preceding the hearing. The disposition of the judge was that she should live with an aunt and uncle in another city nearby.

Another chapter began. "They were so bitter. All I ever heard from them was how awful my mom was. They spent most of their time discussing this, or threatening me that I had better not be like her. I couldn't stand this. So I brought myself back to the court and asked that I be placed somewhere where I could be happy. I never really knew where I wanted to be, but I did know where I didn't want to be! I was willing to trust the court. I knew I would grow up someday and could make my own way. I was so glad I could come to the court and get the help I needed. I didn't want to blame anyone. I could understand I was a burden and that probably my aunt and uncle took me out of a sense of duty. I know it won't always be that way."

Wendi always expressed appreciation for the help others gave her. She was never bitter. It was as she said — she needed a home, now. She would trust the court's judgment, she would do her best, and one day she would grow up and be able to provide for herself. She was always positive in her declaration that she intended to have a home and children, to have a family who belonged to her and to whom she belonged!

As the days passed, a bond grew between us that allowed for freedom of expression. As Wendi reviewed her past life with me and discussed her hopes and plans for the future, I was able to discuss with her her need for the Lord. In her gentle way she was responsive. She indicated a sincere desire to know more and promised that when placed she would attend Sunday school and church. She knew of God and Jesus Christ. But she had never heard of His personal love and concern for her. This overwhelmed her. Wendi was responsive to love, and as I discussed with her the love of the Savior, I knew she would respond if not deterred by human forces. I prayed that she would not experience more heartache before she came to know the Lord, for I knew that in Him she would find the love, the strength, the understanding and the courage to be the "more than conqueror" she so desired to be.

Wendi's probation officer was a source of encouragement to her. Mrs. Brown was a matronly lady with a pleasant, warm approach to children which allowed them to respond without threat. She spent much time with Wendi, including her in the planning of each step in order to prevent any apprehension that someone might once again be planning something she was not aware of.

"Please rise!"

My thoughts returned to the present as the court clerk came through the door, announcing the entrance of the judge.

"You may be seated. Court is in session!"

Before the judge could seat himself, and before Wendi thought of seating herself, she beamed at him and said "Hi!"

"Well, hello, Wendi," greeted the judge and holding out his hand to shake hands with her, he asked, "How are you?"

"Just fine, Your Honor. How are you!"

If any one other than Wendi had been so familiar with the judge, it would have been offensive. But here was a radiant fifteen year old, oblivious to everyone and everything in the room, greeting a friend — His Honor, the judge!

"I am fine, too, Wendi, and it is good to see you. How are things going?"

"Well, Your Honor." Wendi had seated herself. "Things have been great and I know they will be. People have been so nice to me, and this is a nice place, too. I want to thank you for letting me stay here."

The judge looked at her. It was good to see the softness rather than the stern expression so often necessary in the court. His voice betrayed his tenderness as he replied, "Wendi, let me say something to you. It has been a pleasure to have you here. I have had nothing but good reports from the staff, the houseparents, the teachers — from everyone. We are going to miss you. And I want to wish you well. I know you will always make a contribution wherever you are."

The silence in the room was deafening. All eyes were focused on a silvery haired judge, with all authority and power of the state vested in him to do as he chose with this young life, and a willowy, wispy, vibrant fifteen year old who had captivated his heart!

"I understand we are here today to authorize a new home for you," said the judge, "and I am sure Mrs. Brown has done her very best to make an appropriate selection. I understand there could have been other placements, but she did what she thought was best — after discussing it with you, of course."

"I'm sure she did," stated Wendi. "She has been so good to me."

"Mrs. Brown," the judge addressed the probation officer, "what is your plan for this young lady?"

"Your Honor," began Mrs. Brown, "I have a placement for Wendi in a group home here in the city. She will be able to remain there until she is eighteen. She will be attending Linwood High. I am sure they will love her as much as we love her, and that she will get along just fine."

"Well," said Judge Simms, "I am sure she will get along fine, but I am not so sure they will love her as much as we do! When will she be going?"

"This afternoon, Your Honor," replied Mrs. Brown. "I will take her over as soon as you sign the order."

"If this is what you want, Wendi, then this is what we will do. I want you to know we have appreciated your attitude and willingness to work with us. I don't need to tell you to do your best. I know you will. Let us hear from you."

"I will," promised Wendi, "and thank you so much." She stood and held out her hand. The judge took it, and for a moment he looked at Wendi.

"Just stay the way you are, Wendi, don't change, and everything will work out one day. You will see." And with that statement he left the room.

Wendi left that afternoon for group placement. Her new home was nice and comfortable. She shared it with houseparents and ten other girls. She was the youngest resident. Some of the residents were delinquent girls. By contrast, Wendi was a wholesome, unworldly fifteen year old. Hopefully, the influence of these girls would not be so strong that she would take on their way of life.

Enrollment at Linwood High allowed Wendi the opportunity to meet once again adults who really cared and were concerned for her well being. She endeared herself to the administration, to the counseling staff, and to teachers alike. She was particularly fond of one counselor who was a great help to her. This lady was sensitive to Wendi's needs and counseled with her regarding emotional and social developmental phases of her life. Wendi needed a mother's help, and it was good she seemed to always have nearby some older woman who really cared. One of the administrators was also of much help to her. Wendi worked in the office during one period each day and in that way became well acquainted with the administrative staff.

Wendi occasionally visited in our home, but because we had grown very fond of her, and others had the responsibility of caring for her and directing her life, it seemed advisable that we not keep such close contact, but remain friends, keeping in touch with her personally at times, but more often through others. Wendi did attend Sunday school and church with us on several occasions. When I had reason to be in her school and saw her, she was always so happy to see me and was always very loving toward me. She thought a great deal of my husband, and the times we visited with her, she showed her appreciation for his concern for her. Very simply, we loved Wendi and wanted the very best for her. Because we knew she could not be torn between people or personal loyalties, there came a time when we felt it best to withdraw and assume the role of interested adults, never allowing her to really know just how important she was to us. We claimed her for the Lord, and asked that He have our paths cross at His convenient time and use us in any way He so desired in the life of this lovely young lady.

Wendi made good grades in school. She was caught up in the life of the group home, but she had her standards and did not take up with the ways of the delinquent girls. She had plans for college, but she seemed to be frightened as her eighteenth birthday drew nearer. She had resumed the friendship with the neighbor boy of her first foster parents, the first love of her life, and they were married on Christmas Eve, just three days after she was eighteen. Wendi and her husband had a lovely first home. He had a good job. Two beautiful daughters were added, and Wendi had her home at last. She truly belonged, and she was needed by others.

She appeared on television with me on one occasion to tell her story. The emphasis of the program was the need for the young dependent person to have interaction with adults who really cared. She used as examples the people — social workers, her probation officer, the school people, her friends in the community — who really cared enough to take time to meet her needs.

I had a long conversation with Wendi just recently. Once again she shared some of her feelings. One thing that really hurt her was her feeling about being dependent. "I always fought dependency! You know why? The attitude of most people toward dependents is 'you are a part of just a bad bunch of apples.' Stereotyped, that's what dependents really are in the minds of most people, when the idea should be, this is a child with needs, a human being who needs other human beings to have his needs met."

Wendi is as beautiful today as she was at fifteen. She has deep feelings. She is sensitive to the needs of others and to her own needs. She has been reunited with her brother, and they are enjoying a wonderful relationship. She is working in a responsible position at Linwood High where she once attended school. Wendi often states to me, "I believe you would be surprised just how much faith I do have. I know the Lord is not through with me yet."

I wholeheartedly agree.

Chapter 7

Child abuse takes many forms — physical and emotional. Psychological damage is often the result. Fortunately, a few children are able to recognize what is happening and appeal to the court for help. Such is the case of Liz. Not every ending is as happy as this one. While you will be in agreement with the disposition, think about the alternate possibilities and about the future of all the members of this painful situation.

LIZ . . .

"An angel for a mother."

If ever there was a cover girl, Liz was it! She had such a wholesome, All American Girl look! Her flawless complexion complemented her long, well-groomed hair. Graceful, with a smile that won the hearts of all, Liz was an exceptional girl. She communicated in such a refreshing manner in conversation with peers and adults alike. She had time for everyone, for anyone who cared to share a few moments with her. Her school record indicated superior ability. A sophomore in high school, Liz aspired to work with people—"youth work in some Christian organization, or a church" was her way of explaining. "I love people, and I would especially like to work with young people and their families. Families are so important—especially to young people!"

As she seated herself, facing the chair where the judge would sit, Liz looked confident and relaxed. Had someone not acquainted with the juvenile court entered the room, he would have questioned why one with Liz' appearance was seated here, waiting for court to begin. Liz had not been known to the court very long. Her aunt and uncle brought her to the court when she left her home and went to theirs. Liz had been in residence at the Hall for about two weeks. The probation officer had done a comprehensive investigation of her case with the hope of working things out without the court hearing. Her efforts had been in vain. It would now be up to the judge to decide Liz' future, at least for the next few years.

Liz turned to say "hi" to the attorney who was representing her at the order of the court. She smiled as if to say "I have confidence in all of you working with me." Turning to her probation officer who had entered the court room with her, she asked, "Have my folks arrived?"

"I think they will be in shortly. I will see if they are here," answered Miss McGuire. They exchanged smiles as Miss McGuire left the room. She returned a few moments later followed by Liz' father and stepmother.

"They are here," said Miss McGuire, after she had seated the parents. "Would you like to say anything to them before His Honor comes in?"

Liz turned to look at her parents. Her expression showed deep concern. She rose slowly and went to them. "How are you?" she asked.

"What do you care?" asked her stepmother.

"Now, listen," her father turned to his wife and rebuked, "don't you start that stuff here. If you were what you should be, we wouldn't be here."

"What do you mean?" his wife lashed back. "You better take a good look at yourself!"

"Please," pleaded Liz, "not here — please!" She returned to her seat. Sitting straight, head held high, Liz regained her serenity and composure.

In the few weeks Liz had been in the Hall, I had been able to converse with her and review her record. Liz was the daughter of a hardworking man, presently employed as a longshoreman. His hours were long and his work was heavy. He made good money and the family seemed to have the material benefits essential to meet their needs. Liz' mother had passed away three years ago, leaving Liz and two small brothers for the father to care for. Not long after, he remarried. His present wife was some years younger than Liz' mother had been. She had never been around children, and seemed to resent the attention her husband showed his daughter. She also resented Liz' capability. The two younger children seemed to adjust fairly well.

Liz was in the eighth grade when her mother died — a crucial time for her. "I really missed my mother ... we used to have long talks ... but I knew she wanted me to help dad. She had always let me work in the kitchen with her. I knew what dad like to eat, and so I had no problem with the cooking. I had dinner ready when dad would come home." She laughed. "Sometimes it really wasn't too tasty, but dad always told me how good it was. We managed, I thought, but I know dad could see the things that were not being done. The kids' clothes needed mending. I couldn't iron like mom did, and sometimes they really didn't look as nice as they should. I didn't get their hair cut when they needed it. I know I let them eat things they shouldn't. After a time, they began to get sick once in a while, and I would have to miss school to take care of them. The house began to look cluttered, and things were not like mom had them. Dad looked at it all one night and calling me over, he asked how I would like to have some help. I told him I would, because I was tired. I know if I had not begged him to let me try to keep house, he would have hired someone to come in sooner. But after that night he did hire Mary. She came to live in and had one of the boys' rooms. The kids moved in together and I kept my room. At first, we all loved Mary. In no time she had things straightened out. The clothes were clean, the house was clean; we even worked in the yard together. Dad began to relax and when he came home evenings, he and the boys and I had fun again. Some evenings we would go for ice cream cones, or he would take us to buy a record, or maybe some shoes — anything we might need or sometimes anything we just wanted. Mary didn't go with us at first, but then later, the boys seemed to want her to come, so dad asked her to. I had to sit in the back seat then. She sat in the front. It seemed strange to see her next to dad — where mom used to sit. Somehow, when she was not there it was easier to accept the fact that mom was gone. But it was difficult for me to see her in mom's place. I really prayed about that and I knew it was wrong to feel that way. I was determined to make her feel welcome and to do my part. I found that soon I enjoyed having her with us and I thought she enjoyed us.

"Soon Mary was spending every evening with us, doing the things we did, and having a lot of conversation with my dad, advising him about us, sounding as though she really did love us and wanted the best for us. Dad seemed really comfortable having Mary take care of us. One day he told me how thankful he was that he did not have to worry about us, knowing Mary was there. I agreed with him. I didn't have to wash clothes, iron, mend, and do the cooking. Mary never let me work in the kitchen with her. I was not allowed to do any of the cooking. I began to spend a great deal of the time in my own room, doing my studies, cleaning my room, and praying. I knew Mary did not like me, but she did not let my dad know this. Her attitude toward me convinced me of this. She would not talk with me when dad was not around, and then when he was, she never directly spoke to me, but included me with the boys. Every night she gave dad a full report of what had happened that day. Nothing ever went wrong, according to her. I can see why my dad began to feel so good about her. Mary and my dad began to spend a lot of time together after we went to bed. They even went out to dinner without us. When she first came to live with us, she said she didn't care much for church so she stayed home and fixed Sunday dinner while we went, but soon she started going with us .... My mom was a real Christian; so is my dad. He says only the Lord kept him going when mom died .... We always sat together in church, and it really seemed strange to have Mary sitting with us. At first, she let me sit by my dad and she sat next to the boys. But soon that changed and she was sitting next to dad. I know I was jealous, but I prayed about that too, and soon I could accept it. I don't think it would have been so hard if she had been friends with me. But I knew she was not.

"Mom had been gone about a year when dad called us together as a family. He and Mary had something to talk over with us, he said. You might know. They wanted to get married. My heart froze within me, but I thought how selfish I was. I wanted so badly to tell my dad how things really were, but I thought it was just that I was jealous and I did not want to hurt him. He seemed so happy! The boys thought the idea was great. I told dad I wanted what he wanted. Mary gave me a quick, dirty look, but dad was not aware of it. So, they were married. I felt sure Mary and I would be friends once they were married, but it didn't work out that way. They went away for a few days and when they came home, she moved her things into dad's room. The next day she said she wanted to speak with me. Dad was at work.

'I want you to know,' she said, 'I am in charge here! The sooner you understand that, the better off you will be. I will take no foolishness from you. I have the right now to run this house, and I will. You ask me from here on out when you want something, or want to do something. Here is a list of the work you will be responsible for, and I do not want to hear any complaints or you will hear from me. Do you have that straight?'

"I assured her that I did and took the list. Wow! What was she going to do? When I got home from school each day, there was a long list of things to do — the washing, ironing, and most of the supper. She would come into the kitchen shortly before my dad got home and take the credit for what had been done. It was all I could do to keep up. Mary sat, ordering me around, and if I did not do the job the way she felt it should be done, she would slap me across the head or face. The boys became tense and upset. I was so miserable I couldn't eat. One night the boys and I asked to speak with our dad. We told him what had been going on. He was shocked! When he went to Mary, she denied everything and convinced him I was making it all up. Dad had a long talk with us then. He told us how much having Mary meant to him, and how he hoped we would work with her. He said he knew we missed mom, but that we had to live today. I felt terrible and told him we would try. The next day after school I went home to find Mary had really whipped the boys for what they said to dad. When I came in she had a belt in her hand:

" 'It is your turn now. You will learn who is the boss here.'

"She really whipped me too. We didn't tell dad, but that night he seemed concerned because we were so quiet. Our home became a very unhappy place to be. One night dad asked us to come in. Mary was in the living room with him. He said he knew something was wrong and the only way to deal with it was to get it out in the open. At first we were scared. Then I thought I would tell him all that had been going on. I started at the beginning and went over it. The boys agreed with me. Mary was not so mean to them, but they saw how she treated me and if they defended me, they got a licking too. My dad was horrified. He turned on Mary. She denied this and said we were trying to get rid of her. I showed dad the belt marks then. He grabbed her and for a moment I thought he would hit her.

" 'You pack your things and leave,' he said.

"Mary pleaded. We asked dad to let her stay. Maybe we were wrong, but it did make things easier for dad to have someone take care of us.

"Things went along pretty well for about a week. Dad began to relax a little and we thought things would be all right. But they were not. Somehow Mary had built her case. My dad kind of turned on me. He told me he really thought I was against him and Mary and that he wanted me to know she was in charge and that he would deal with me if I did not cooperate. I was so surprised, but what could I say? A real hassle developed. Dad would come home. Mary would complain about me. Dad would lash out at me and I began to lash back. Mary beat me. Dad was right in the big middle. They argued so much, everything was just awful. The boys cried a lot, and did not feel well. Dad would threaten to get rid of Mary one minute and in the next threaten to punish me and the boys. I knew something had to be done. I left and went to my aunt and uncle's home. I told them the whole story and they believed me. My dad came over and said he was taking me home. We got into a big hassle. I refused to return if Mary were there. He demanded I return home. I refused. My dad finally said he would call the police and they would take me home. My uncle said he would not allow that. He told my dad he would bring me to the Hall and let the court decide what to do. Although my dad was very upset and angry with all of us, that is what my uncle did. I filed my own petition, and I do not want to return to my home. I am worried about my little brothers, but I just can't take it any longer."

During the days Liz was in the Hall, her father visited her. The probation officer spoke with them, attempting to reconcile the family. Apparently Mary was able to tell a convincing story and for about a week the father vacillated between his wife and daughter, not knowing which was right, believing one at times, the other at times. But he was convinced that Liz was telling the truth when he went home one night and found that the two boys had run to the neighbor's following a beating from Mary. There must have been a horrible row in the home when Liz' dad discovered the abuse of the boys. Mary's things were packed and she was asked to leave the home.

"Dad and the boys have been trying to make it by themselves, but they don't ... they can't," said Liz. "I really don't know what to do!" She seemed confused momentarily. "But the Lord knows what to do." She smiled, and her personal faith seemed to rejuvenate her and once again she was her radiant self.

The court room door opened and Liz saw her aunt and uncle enter the room. She smiled at them. Her aunt came to her, whispering reassurance in her ear. Liz kissed her — there was evident affection between them. Her aunt was the sister of her mother and Liz often spoke of how fond she was of her and how like her mother her aunt was. Taking her seat beside her husband, the aunt reached for his hand and they sat giving the appearance of a united front in defense of the lovely girl. Liz' dad moved to sit with them, leaving Mary alone.

"Well, how about that! For two cents I would leave!" Mary exclaimed. She received only disapproving glances from the three adults.

"Please rise!"

The court clerk had entered the room, the juvenile court judge following her. With brisk steps he approached his chair and seated himself.

As the judge rested his eyes on Liz, his face softened. Glancing around the room, he became aware of the division of the family, and a stern look returned to his face.

Mary sat angrily shifting in her seat. Before the judge could speak she blurted out, "I don't know why I am here ... everything has been decided. I don't have a chance. I would like to go!"

"We will have no outbursts in this court," the judge stated. "You are here because you have been served with a notice and summons to appear. You will remain until this court dismisses you and there will be no further comments until you are directed to speak. Is that clear?"

"I don't want to be here. I don't like this girl, and I have been ordered out of the house. I don't see any reason why I have to be here when I am not even one of them. I don't want to be mixed up with trash like this."

Liz' dad was on his feet.

"Wait just a minute! Don't you call my daughter trash."

Mary was on her feet and for a moment it appeared there would be open, physical conflict.

"Oh, please," said Liz, "not here, Dad, please sit down." She had gone to him, and was hugging him and pleading.

"It is all right. The judge will handle it." The probation officer went to Liz and brought her back to her seat. Liz' father sat down, visibly shaken. He put his handkerchief over his face and wept. His sister in law attempted to comfort him. The judge waited momentarily for order. "The next person to disrupt this court will be cited for contempt and will go to jail. Is that clear?" The silence indicated that it was.

"Now," the judge picked up the petition, "if we can have some respect and order this court will begin." The petition was read. Liz was asking the court to allow her to live somewhere other than her home, preferably with her aunt and uncle. She declared in her petition that her home life, since her father's remarriage, had become unbearable and she felt she could no longer live there. "How does your client plead, regarding her case?" the judge asked the guardian ad litem.

"Your Honor, Liz insists she cannot live at home as long as her stepmother is there. She indicates she cannot tolerate the fighting and the confusion, and that she is emotionally upset over this. She told me prior to the court hearing that she felt her dad had made some changes since she was entered at the Hall by her uncle, and she states this may change the picture some. I have not had opportunity to speak with her father, but can speak for Liz in saying that she refuses to live in the same house with her stepmother. The probation officer has the latest information regarding the status of the home and I think it advisable to hear from her," concluded the attorney.

The judge looked at the probation officer. "Miss McGuire?"

"Yes, Your Honor. Things have changed somewhat since the petition was signed. Liz' father has separated from the stepmother, who is now out of the home. Mr. Owen assures me he wants his daughter home. I believe there is a great deal of love between Liz and her father. Liz is a capable girl and she wants to do the right thing, but she cannot handle the situation with her stepmother. Liz is honest and forthright, and is really an exceptional girl. I don't know what Mr. Owen's immediate plans are, but he did tell me yesterday he would like to have all three of his children at home. His mother is coming from the east coast to help out until he can hire an older lady to assist in the household responsibilities and to look after the children." This was news to Liz. She turned to her father and her smile almost said a loud "thank you!"

"Mr. Owen," said the judge. "I want to hear from you. What has been going on?"

Mr. Owen rose to his feet. "Your Honor, I would like to apologize to the court for my outburst and I want you to know, Sir, I know better. I am just upset! I want to apologize to my daughter for ever doubting her word. I love her deeply. And I want to apologize to her aunt and uncle and thank them for taking things into their own hands until I could come to my senses. I guess I wanted a home for my children so badly I forgot there are important issues to consider. I acted impulsively without really listening and observing too much. I really made a mess of things, but I think I have it together now. My mother will be here this afternoon. She will stay as long as I need her. Liz is a very capable girl and she can help her grandmother with everything when I am not home. My little boys are sick — emotionally troubled. They are at their aunt and uncle's home now. This has been a horrible thing, and all because I thought I was doing what was best for my children. If the court will let me, I want to take my daughter home. I love her. If her mother were here ..." his voice choked.

Liz wiped the tears from her eyes. There was silence in the room. Mr. Owen took his seat.

"Mr. Owen, don't be too hard on yourself. We all make mistakes, and while we are human, we will continue to do so."

"Yes?" the judge said to Mrs. Owen who had raised her hand.

"Do you think I might be allowed to say something — I am a part of this family, you know!" Her voice dripped with sarcasm.

"What do you have to say? I must warn you, no outbursts," the judge added.

"Well, in the first place," began Mrs. Owen, "I worked my head off for these people. I gave up my home, moved in with them, and worked like a dog! Those kids are the most ungrateful bunch I have ever met, and Liz is a real snip! She can convince her dad of anything and he swallows it, hook, line, and sinker! And as far as being ordered out, I left. I don't need them! I had a good life before I met them and I can have it again. I just wish I had another opportunity — I would beat some sense into that girl's head. She is a real trouble-maker, believe me."

Mr. Owen was on his feet.

"Your Honor, I apologize to the court again, but I cannot listen to this any longer. This is a pack of lies! These children kept all of their feelings to themselves for days before I ever heard of it. Then I would not believe them until Liz showed me the marks of the belt on her back. Later the boys were beaten severely and ran from home to a neighbor's house before I was finally convinced. Liz admits she was jealous, but I know my daughter. I think she worked that out and really tried. I know kids need discipline, but they don't need cruel treatment. We never had arguing and fighting in our home when their mother was alive." He faltered a moment, then continued. "She trained the children well. She was gentle, a real lady, and she taught Liz to be a responsible young lady. After she died, Liz and I tried to make it alone. That little girl worked hard and kept up her grades too. The only reason I hired this woman to come into our home was to prevent my little daughter from killing herself. It was too much. Then I got carried away. This woman is a sly one. She really gave me a snow job. Then, when she got me to marry her she showed her true colors. I have sure been stupid. I want my children home. They belong there and deserve a home. If I can't have them, their aunt and uncle are here to give them a home. We love these children. All of us do, and they belong to me. I would do anything to have Liz back with me." Mr. Owen sat again.

"Liz, what do you have to say?" asked the judge.

Liz sat for a moment to gain composure. Those in the room, including Liz, had been touched deeply by her father's remarks. "I have always known I was loved by my parents. When mom was here, both of them loved me so much — together. When mom died, dad sort of tried to double his love. We have never doubted he loved us. I am not surprised to hear my dad say what he did. I knew it before he said it. He has been hurt so badly. I am sorry I was a part of it . . ." she choked and continued . . . "I want to be with my dad and my brothers, but I cannot stand fighting and arguing and lies. We have not been brought up that way. I can't live that way."

Mr. Owen was on his feet again. "Your Honor, may I stand by my daughter?"

"Yes, you may, Mr. Owen. Come forward!"

Mr. Owen went to his daughter's side. He placed his arm around her shoulder. Patting her gently he said, "There, there, honey, don't worry. It will be all right."

Liz leaned against him. Observing them together, the court appeared convinced there was nothing more to worry about. The detour had been painful, but adversity would contribute to the strength and growth of this family in the days ahead.

"The petition will be dismissed. Liz, go home with your father. These have been trying days, I am sure, but I think it is over. I know you have each learned from these experiences."

"And you, Mrs. Owen," he addressed the stepmother, "I hope you have learned also. This man entrusted his dearest possessions to you — his children — and you abused them. I have no respect for anyone who will abuse children. You had the opportunity to be a part of a deep experience, that of guiding and directing the lives of three children in addition to sharing the life of a sincere man. Apparently, you didn't have what it takes. You could be charged with child abuse if this man were so inclined. I hope you have learned from this experience and that I won't see you in court again some day charged with beating either your child or that of another."

"Mr. Owen," the judge held out his hand. "You are a fortunate man. You came to your senses! Take your children, and take them home. Love them as you have. I wish you well, sir! Liz, stay just the way you are. I hope we hear from you again, but not officially! I wish you well. Take good care of your dad and your brothers, and Liz, enjoy your grandmother. Grandmothers are very special people, too. I know. I am a grandfather, so I know one personally."

With a twinkle in his eye and a smile on his face, the judge left the court room. Liz and her father embraced. The uncle and aunt rushed to their side. The stepmother watched them for a moment and then said, "Boy, have I ever been put down, and after all I did. This is sure some gratitude! You guys stink!" and with that she left the court room.

Liz went home. Grandmother arrived, and the family settled in to good, wholesome routine family life — a lot of love, seasoned with appropriate discipline. The children regained their trust and confidence, and blossomed and grew. Mr. Owen was himself again. Grandmother had been alone in the east and needed a home too, so the arrangement became more or less a permanent thing — "Unless Josh decides to marry again," she exclaimed with a twinkle in her eye.

"I don't think so..." Josh spoke as though he were thinking aloud. "Sometimes I get so lonely, I miss her so (speaking of his first wife) I can hardly bear it. But then I look at the children. I have so much, and I am so thankful. She would be pleased with the way they are growing up. They are such good kids. But, then, they had an angel for a mother!"

Chapter 8

Incorrigible petitions, as they are called, are most often filed by parents of children who are unmanageable in the home. There is a fine line between incorrigibility and true dependency, in that incorrigible children are usually neglected in some way. The question is, why is the child acting out? Is he reacting to a living situation that is not conducive to healthful development? Is the interaction with the parent such that growth is psychologically impaired? Must he be rescued from his own family?

The incorrigible child is usually, but not always, a rebellious child. He is at odds with himself, his home, and often with a segment of the community. He resists controls not only in the home, but often from authority at any level. He is usually headstrong, self-willed, and self-centered.

The judge appears to have a difficult time with such cases. Because he sees the family as a unit, and knows the actions of one influence the others, he cannot separate the behavior of the child from that of the influence of the home.

To the child who appears to be the victim of circumstances, he may say, "Get it together. Despite the raw deal you have had in life, there comes a time when you must make it on your own. You are growing up. Stand on your own two feet!" In making disposition of a case where the child was uncooperative, the judge asked, "Do I have to hit you with a baseball bat to get your attention? Or put a ring in your nose and lead you around by it? You can't just work hard a week before a court hearing. That is like taking a dose of castor oil! Why not work hard before? You prove things by doing them, not by saying what you plan to do!"

Not all incorrigibles are openly defiant, rude, or rebellious. Many of these children know how to behave, and they demonstrate so in court. To find a young man or young lady following the hearing, shaking hands with the probation officer or guardian ad litem, thanking him, is not uncommon. They have, at one time or another, had good training. For these, separation from the family is never for long.

Once again, the court room scene brings forth compelling evidence. You be the observer. Listen carefully to Bart's story. Follow the investigation as it unfolds. Weight the words and actions of the parents. Decide for yourself. Was this easy for any one? Does any one win?

BART ...

"A home is more than rooms separated by walls."

The court hearing was being delayed. The attorney appointed as guardian ad litem for Bart had asked for the delay, in order to have opportunity to speak with the parents of the boy who was to be before the court on an incorrigible petition. Bart had been seated in the court room for several minutes and was becoming quite restless. The probation officer had brought him in and had left to attempt to determine when the hearing would start. It had been a long day. There had been several hearings preceding this and everyone seemed tired. So was Bart. As the time drew near, he showed signs of tension and fatigue. Since there were few people in the court room, he rose and went to the window behind the judge's chair. Outside the exotic birds were making their usual noise; the sounds had attracted Bart's attention.

Turning to the court reporter in the room he asked, "What kinds of birds are those?"

"I really don't know," answered the man. He rose and joined Bart at the window. They chatted together as they watched the birds.

"Where did they git 'um?" asked Bart.

"I think different organizations donated them," replied the reporter. "Their wings were clipped so they could not fly out of the court yard. They are pretty, but they surely do make a lot of noise. During the last hearing it was kind of loud."

"Yeah," said Bart, "what did the judge do?"

"Oh, nothing, he just kept on with the hearing. Some of the people in the court room sort of grinned, but the judge acted like he didn't hear them."

The two stood silently watching the antics of the fowl. At last the reporter went back to his chair and Bart also came slowly back and seated himself. "Wonder what is keeping them?" he inquired of the reporter.

"I don't know," came the answer, "but here is Mr. Blair; maybe he can tell you."

Mr. Blair, the probation officer in this case, took his seat directly behind and to the right of Bart. "Mr. Blair, what's holding it up?' asked Bart.

"Your attorney is speaking with your parents. He hopes to convince them that you should go home. What do you think of that?" asked Mr. Blair.

"I don't know." Bart hung his head. "I don't think they will let me, they are pretty mad."

"Well, he can only try," said Mr. Blair. "That is what you want, isn't it?"

"Yeah," said Bart, "but they won't buy it." He continued to sit, eyes downcast as though in deep thought.

The guardian ad litem entered the court room, looking flustered. He went over to Bart. "I can't make them agree, Bart. They just feel that they have had it. They say they can't believe you any longer, so I guess it is up to the judge to rule now."

"I thought that would be what they would say," answered Bart. He continued to look down. The attorney took his place. Nervously working a pencil between his hands, he looked expectantly toward the chamber door which would open momentarily to allow the judge to enter.

"Bart," the probation officer was speaking, "would you like to speak with your parents? You may sit with them for a few minutes, at least until the judge comes in."

Bart shook his head. His parents were seated behind him. They could not see his face; he wiped a tear from his eyes and swallowed hard a couple of times. Then, as though he had decided it was up to him to prove that he was a man, he raised his head, turned to his attorney and said, "It's okay, I deserve it!"

Bart had been entered at the Hall by his father as an incorrigible child four days prior to the hearing. That particular evening he had been allowed to attend a dinner at a friend's and had come home under the influence of some kind of controlled substance, in addition to alcohol. His parents were furious. They indicated to the intake officer that they had warned Bart of the consequences of such behavior — that he would be entered at the Hall if he disobeyed.

The record reflected that Bart and his parents had experienced a harrowing year. Bart was a junior in high school. He had been an athlete, had made good grades, but for some reason he and his parents could not work things out regarding his extracurricular activities. His social life, according to his parents, left much to be desired, and now as a junior he was beginning to keep late hours, drink, and use some kind of drugs.

Bart was one of two children. An older sister had graduated from high school with honors, had received a scholarship, and was in her first year at the state university. She had never given her parents a moment's worry. She never dated, was completely lost in her studies, was always obedient, enjoyed the same things her parents did. To her brother she was "a real dud ... cold fish!" When the two were younger, Bart's sister always found a way to avoid conflict. "She never would stick up for her rights," said Bart. "I could take anything of hers I wanted, do what I wanted to her, and she would never tell on me, or fight back. I think she was afraid for the folks to know she had feelings. I never could have a good fight with her, and I never could talk with her. Some of the guys say they talk to their sisters, man, they get dates for them and things like that ... wow, she never dated herself! She was far out ... weird!"

Mr. and Mrs. Chadwick, according to the report, saw their daughter's behavior as the result of their competent training. They could not understand the threat that Bart presented to their standard of living, family structure, and even to their reputation. Mr. Chadwick indicated in his conference with the probation officer that he had been in some difficulty with legal authorities when he was a young adult, and that one of his brothers had served some time in a distant state for auto theft. He said he knew first hand the trouble Bart could get into, and would not allow him to be disobedient in the home. He also stated that his wife was not aware of his youthful pranks, and he wanted to spare her that. He certainly did not want their son to turn sour and ruin the family.

Mrs. Chadwick confided to the probation officer that she and her husband were not the kind of parents who found it easy to share themselves with the children, or even with each other. She said she felt that there had always been a "certain distance between us all" that had created the feeling of not knowing one another too well. She characterized her husband as a good provider, a very organized, cautious man, sometimes fearful of business involvements, and highly competitive. Although she felt herself of a good background, she found her husband's way of life a little conservative, and wished at times that he were able to relax and spend a few hours in fun.

Mr. Chadwick saw his wife as supportive and enjoying life with him. He indicated that she "never questions my rules" and "does well by us all ... clothes are always washed and ironed, food on the table ... good housekeeper!"

The rules of the home regarding Bart's social interaction with other young people had not been developed consistently, but were decided at the moment. Bart told the probation officer that he was to ask his father each time he wanted to leave the home. He did not object to this, but he never knew whether he would be granted permission or not. This seemed to depend on the mood of his father. He was not allowed to consult his mother, though he doubted if she would be any different. On one occasion attending a game might be allowed, whereas on the next it might be forbidden. As a result, Bart could not make any plans, and frankly admitted his frustration and his resentment towards his parents. At seventeen Bart could not answer his friends, if asked to join them at a game or party. He had no choice in deciding. The answer came from his father. If the answer was no, there was no further discussion. If yes, a long list of lengthy rules was added. "It really wasn't worth it most of the time, I always ended up in trouble, and he was always waiting when I got home to let me know it. Three minutes late meant ... well, weeks of restriction. I just got fed up!"

A conversation with Bart before the hearing revealed the following account of facts leading up to today. Bart had spent much of the year on restriction. He had had to give up sports, which hurt. His grades began to drop and he seemed to lose interest. "I thought, what's the use. I might as well live it up when I get the chance. I guess I took it too far."

On several occasions Bart's father had used physical force, and although Bart had never struck his father he admitted that he was tempted. "He's not a bad guy ... but man, he can sure make it rough. Mom just sits like my sister did, and never says anything. It's just dad and me at one another's throats."

"If I wanted to," continued Bart, "I could snow him. I could play his game and I don't think he would know the difference. But I know that wouldn't be right. You know, I really don't think that I would do anything all that bad if they just trusted me a little, but it's a bummer ... and no fun, no way!

"I recall when I was a little guy," Bart looked back. "Dad never did play with me, you know, ball and all that stuff you read about. If I played ball it was with my friends and their dads. Once in awhile I got to go out with friends, maybe to a picnic, or skating. Sometimes whole families would go and they would take me. I can remember they always had to leave early because dad set such crazy hours for me. I always felt like I spoiled their fun. When I was a little kid I really didn't think about it, but when I got older, say eleven or twelve, I saw what was happening. I just quit going, no need to spoil it for everybody else.

"Well, with so much time, it was either study or do nothing. For awhile I got busy with school work and was in some sports. Then my dad got to where if I made a C he would blow his stack. I had to keep the grades up. It was really hard. Sometimes I tried hard and couldn't get it. Boy, did I catch it!

"Then I got into high school. I was pretty good in basketball and dad was sort of proud of that. He never did come to the games. If I didn't make the points, though, he would say he was going to pull me off the team. That got old. I sort of goofed around, skipped some practices, and soon wasn't doing too well with sports. This year the coach warned me, and I would have made it, but dad restricted me so often I had to drop. One night, just before a game, he decided I couldn't go play because I had forgotten to take the garbage out that morning. I guess that did it. I threw in the towel the next day, and told the coach I was through. Personally, I think he was relieved. He had a team to work with, and I was beginning to be a drag.

"I skipped school a few times and went over to a friend's house. He had some marijuana. We smoked some and it felt good. It seemed like my troubles kind of faded away. I began to find ways of buying my own. I took some of my mom's money from her purse. I knew that she wouldn't tell my dad. She never let on she missed it. She's like that ... just like my sister, never says anything. I don't like that. I felt guilty, but I sure liked the marijuana, so I took some more. After that she never left any money in her purse. So I sold a few of my things, bummed from others, and kept smoking it once in awhile.

"One day my friend asked me if I really wanted to feel good. I said 'sure'. He gave me some acid. Wow! Did I ever spin! But I couldn't let on I didn't like it. I didn't go back there for awhile. I really was kind of scared.

"The night I really blew it I had asked permission to go to a friend's house for dinner. His mother even called my home and asked permission. They were kind of uppity people, so my dad said I could go. I was supposed to be home by ten. We had our dinner, there were several kids there, and then the parents of my friend went out. My friend brought out his folk's liquor and some pills. That's what we had. I really felt kind of sick after taking two or three pills, but I was afraid to say anything, so I just went home.

"I got home a little early, and I thought my parents would be pleased because I had come in before ten. My dad was waiting up as usual. I started up to my bedroom. He called out, 'come on in here and tell us how you enjoyed associating with real people for a change.' I mumbled some excuse, but it didn't work. I had to go into the livingroom. I was sick. My dad said I was drunk and on drugs. He brought me to the Hall. All the way here he said he was not going to have me in the home any longer. He wanted me to live somewhere else and he was going to ask the court to do that. I was too sick to really care. All I could think of was 'let me go to bed.'

"Well, the next morning I asked my probation officer if he would call my folks and ask them to come to see me. He did, and they came. My mom didn't say anything. My dad told me how I had disgraced the family, and that they did not want me home. I tried to tell him what had happened and apologize. He wouldn't listen. I thought 'what's the use anyhow,' so I blew it. I told him what I really thought about how he had treated me all my life and how unfair I thought he was. That did it. He said I was ungrateful, and he was through with me.

"I guess he is unless somebody can convince him I really would like to go home. I have thought about it, and I would really try to please them. I only have a little over a year left, and then off to college. I would like to make it, I really would, if he will let me.

"I guess you are supposed to love your folks. I think that I do love them. Sometimes they seem like strangers. I was over at one of my friend's one day and his mother said to him and his sister, "You guys, you are the greatest, I really love you ... wouldn't trade you for a million." I felt strange. I thought my friend would be embarrassed. Instead he went over to his mother and hugged her and kissed her! Later that same day my friend's dad came home. He kissed all of them! They all seemed so glad to see one another. Then he said to me how glad he was to have me there, shook hands with me and made me feel real welcome. When some of my friends come around here my dad lets it be known very soon that he is on to us and that there will be no horseplay, whatever he means by that. I just don't ask kids over anymore. We don't have any fun at our house. It is always kind of an eerie feeling, like something awful is about to happen.

"My dad makes good money. I don't know what they do with it. They don't go out. They do **ha**ve liquor in the house. He has a drink or two every night. My mom doesn't drink that I know of. She sits and knits or sews. He watches television, reads the paper, and falls asleep in the chair. We never have had other families in. Our relatives don't live around here. We don't ever see them. I never did know my grandparents. I think they died when I was young. I think my mom has some sisters in New York. She gets a Christmas card from them every year. We don't go anywhere. I was thinking in the cell — other kids talk about their vacations ... we have never been on one, you know, and I have never been to a camp. Guess you can't miss what you never had, but I wonder what it would be like."

Conversation with Bart left one emotionally drained. He had suffered so much psychological deprivation it seemed a relief to him to just spew forth his feelings.

His school record indicated that he was no behavior problem. His test scores indicated ability well above average, and his grades up to this year reflected that. This year they dropped. He had, as he said, begun to skip school. The school staff was concerned about his adjustment. According to the record, his parents had not attended any conference or school function.

While Mr. Chadwick seemed to be a responsible businessman and seemed to be doing well in his position, he kept his personal life, including his family, almost isolated from the world. The family did not attend church, except on holidays, and then Mr. Chadwick gave generously to the offering. "He always griped because the preacher didn't write him and thank him for the check," explained Bart. "He said he knew nobody else ever gave as much as he did."

The Chadwick home was in a section of nicer homes. Though not elaborate, it was well built and comfortable. The yard was well kept. Had it not been, Bart would have keenly felt the consequences!

Everyone was growing increasingly restless. What was keeping the judge? Perhaps he too was feeling the strain of the day, and may have taken a coffee break — a well deserved one.

"Please rise!"

The judge entered as all stood to attention. "This court is now in session, you may be seated," directed the court clerk.

"We have a petition here alleging that Bart Chadwick is an incorrigible child as defined by the statutes. The petition is filed by his parents who state that this was necessary. Bart did willfully disobey by attending a dinner party where he drank alcohol and took drugs, returning to the home under the influence of these. The parents further state that for the past year they have been unable to control Bart. He does not follow rules, does not come in when he is supposed to, and participates in activities which are not approved by his parents. The request of the parents is that he not return to the home, but be placed in a group home. What is your position in this, Mr. Simmons?" asked the judge.

"Your Honor, there is no disagreement as to the facts alleged in the petition, with the exception of the disposition. Bart wishes to return home, but we can get to that later," answered Mr. Simmons.

Turning to the probation officer the judge asked for a background report and a recommendation. Mr. Blair gave a comprehensive report outlining the background of the case, including the events of the year which led up to Bart's detention at the Hall. "Your Honor, I would like to see Bart return home. He would like to do this. I believe he has thought things through carefully and realizes that he should be obedient to his parents whether he agrees with them or not. I think that he is ready to do that. This is his first time to be brought to the attention of the court. He was not arrested for breaking the law. This is strictly a family situation, and one which I hope all parties concerned would be willing to look at carefully, honestly evaluating his or her own role, and being willing to take the steps necessary to correct the situation. That is what Bart would like to do, and that is my recommendation."

Before the judge could ask Mr. Chadwick to speak, he was on his feet. "Your Honor, I do not want that boy home! He has deliberately disobeyed me! I will not tolerate that! You can do what you want with him, but don't send him back with me. He drinks, he smokes pot, and now he is using something else — I don't know what. He was in a stupor when he came home, and I have had it. I have provided for him, given him a home, a respectable family, and now I am through. He thinks he is a big man, let him handle it, but leave me out."

"This is some outburst, Mr. Chadwick," stated the judge. "It seems that you have made up your mind without discussing it very thoroughly with anyone. Is that the case?"

"No! I talked it over with Mr. Blair. I told him I did not want Bart back. I also told the attorney that. I think I have given him every chance ... I have been more than fair. He seems to want it this way, so I will give it to him."

"Did you talk it over, Mr. Chadwick, or did you tell them?" asked the judge.

"I talked to them ... and I told them, I don't want him back. He is disobedient." Mr. Chadwick was emphatic in his declaration.

"Mrs. Chadwick, what do you wish to say?" asked the judge.

"She doesn't have anything to say," answered Mr. Chadwick.

"In this court, Mr. Chadwick," said the judge, "she will have her say! Mrs. Chadwick?"

"I will go along with my husband, I have nothing to say," answered Mrs. Chadwick. Her husband smiled.

"Well, you were right on that one, Mr. Chadwick, but you are wrong on so many other counts. You really haven't gained a great deal, I hope you see that," responded the judge. "Now Bart, I would like to hear from you."

"I did what they said. I guess they are right. I would like to go home, but if they don't want me, it wouldn't work." Bart lowered his head.

"Bart," asked the judge, "what is the problem, and what do you think should be done?"

"Your Honor," Bart did not hesitate to speak with the judge, "I have disobeyed, but sometimes I felt really put down by my dad especially. I don't think it is fair the way the rules are set and I don't think he is right when he thinks it won't work. I know it would. I am willing to agree he is in charge. I would like to go home, do as he says, and try to please them. I really do want to go home. I know I will do my part, but I don't think he will let me. I think he has made up his mind, so I guess that is it."

"Is that it, Mr. Chadwick?" asked the judge. "Aren't you willing to take this boy home and try to work this out? If you would all have counseling, try to get to understand one another a little better, it seems to me things would work out. We don't want to see homes broken up. We feel families are better off together. I would like for you to try it."

"No way," said Mr. Chadwick. "I told that boy, and I mean it, and that is final. I don't want him home, do I have to say it any plainer!"

"You have said it plain enough, Mr. Chadwick, plain enough," said the judge. "Bart, I can't send you home. You need to be where you are cared for and where you can receive guidance and instruction. I appreciate your feelings and your willingness to want to work it out, but you can't do it alone. We want you to stay here with us for awhile, and hopefully Mr. Blair can find a suitable placement for you. I know this is hard for you, but I want you to work with us. Will you?"

"Yes sir, I will. I am sorry too, but there is not much that I can do about it," answered Bart.

"I would like for you to leave the room now, Bart," said the judge. "I want to speak with your parents." Bart was directed from the court room by the probation officer who came back and took his seat. When the door was closed behind Bart, the judge turned to the guardian ad litem. "I neglected to ask you what your recommendation was. I was upset by all that I heard. I apologize."

"Your Honor," spoke the attorney, "I can understand your feelings. There is no need for an apology. I spoke with Mr. and Mrs. Chadwick for some time before the hearing. I did my best to get them to give Bart another chance. I got nowhere. I believe Bart is better off not returning there. I don't see this as a suitable placement for Bart."

"That's some statement. What do you mean not a suitable placement! I'll have you know— " Mr. Chadwick did not finish before the judge interrupted.

"Mr. Chadwick, you are out of order. You are in a court. You do not have the control here. You remain silent until you are directed to speak!"

"But I won't have anybody saying anything about me and my home," blurted Mr. Chadwick.

"I shall find you in contempt if there is one more outburst, Mr. Chadwick," reminded the judge. "I agree with the attorney. I am sorry for Bart. Every child would like a home with a mother and a father. A home is more than rooms separated by walls. It is a place where not just food, clothing, and shelter are provided, but where these are wrapped in love, tempered with fair discipline, and where guidance and direction are given by parents who love one another and their children. I don't think this is the case here. I don't feel you can love anyone, not even yourself. If you did, you would do some serious thinking and make some changes.

"I am going to place your son, not because you say so, but because it is best for him. But you, sir, will share the expenses. I have looked over your financial statement, and I shall order you to pay two hundred fifty dollars per month for Bart's care while he is in a group home. I shall review your financial status periodically and increase the amount if it so warrants. So do not do any big spending from now until Bart is out of group care. You might have to return the purchase.

"I can understand a family getting into a situation where there could be problems, but I cannot understand parents not willing to attempt to work through them in order to have a child return home. Well, if Bart doesn't mean enough to you, he does to this court. I am concerned about one thing, and one thing only, and that is what is best for Bart. Right now, you aren't, so he won't be returning home. I hope you get the picture. You, Mr. Chadwick, are the source of your son's problems whether you like it or not. This court is adjourned." The judge rose to his feet and left the room.

"Why, why, who does he think he is?" sputtered Mr. Chadwick.

"He is the judge, sir. Would you like to challenge him?" asked the guardian.

"I won't pay a dime, not one cent for that boy, you will see," blurted Mr. Chadwick.

"I think the judge will consider that a challenge of his authority, Mr. Chadwick. Shall I call him back so that you can tell him that?" asked the attorney.

"Never mind, let's go," and Mr. Chadwick took his wife's arm and left the court room.

Bart lived in group placement until he completed high school. His probation officer heard from him occasionally. His adjustment was satisfactory, but not outstanding.

"He never did get over his parents not letting him return home," Mr. Blair related. "The last I heard he had entered the service. I haven't heard for some time, now. In every letter he sounded lonely, still confused by it all, almost without direction of any kind. I hope he puts it together. But if he does, he will have to do it on his own. I have never in all my years met such cold, uncaring parents."

Chapter 9

Runaway children are a heartache and a headache for all involved. Parents spend agonizing hours wondering whether the child is safe. Visions of finding the body dumped along some lonely road fill their minds. Fear of the child's exposure to drug use, prostitution, and other delinquent acts weighs heavily on their spirits. Hours drag into days and days into weeks with no word from the child. It is a blessed relief to have the police call, announcing that the child is in custody. Perhaps he is miles away, but at least safe in a cell!

To the runaway the judge has special words: "You are living a very selfish life! You are hurting others! If you find you cannot live in your home for one reason or the other, there is a better way to get out! You think you are an adult — mature enough to handle the situation. Let me clue you in: there are things out there bigger than you are!"

Frequently a runaway has been harbored by others. It is possible for a child to be missing for months only to be found a short distance from home.

The judge expresses his concern: "Charges can and should be filed by your parents against these people. It is against the law to harbor a runaway. What price did you pay for your rent? People don't feed you and give you a bed to sleep in without some charge! You probably won't believe this, but this is the first step to living the rest of your life as a criminal. Kids end up drug addicts, prostitutes, burglars, and thieves of every description when they are playing Mr. or Miss Big — living away from home, sheltered by so-called friends! You are being used, and you are not smart enough to see it!"

A child may refuse to return home following a run. The probation officer presents to the court the social file information. His investigation may reveal extreme deprivation or even cruel treatment. When the return home is discussed, the child usually indicates "if you send me home, I will run again ... I can't stand it there! We just can't make it!"

With the hope of possibly uniting the family in the future, the judge attempts to explain to the parents. "If this is the feeling, sending your child home is futile. Don't you agree it would be better if placement were out of the home for a period of time? This would allow all of you to have the opportunity to attempt to reconcile your differences. Before long, you will be together again." Parents usually agree.

The family willing to work toward the goal of being reunited is almost certain to succeed. It is the parent or child who sees no personal responsibility in what has happened, or refuses to work with professional staff, or with one another, that experiences defeat. The result is that the child remains a ward of the state. Placement continues indefinitely.

Foster homes and group homes are scarce, and they are expensive. When room in one is available, someone has to pay the bill. Parents often do not have the financial resources with which to pay. The judge will include in the order, however, a token payment, if nothing more, for the therapeutic value. By sharing in the support of the child, the parents continue to be a part of that life, to be considered in planning at every level. In addition, they have a feeling of self worth in fulfilling the obligation imposed by the court — they cannot be accused of abandonment.

Welfare funds are used to supplement any payment made by the parent for the child. Children in many states are referred to the various social service agencies for placement. Probation officers also work on placement in group settings throughout the state. Wherever the child is placed, it will cost money. Just as institutionalization costs are soaring, so are costs for maintenance in placement. Very few families are able to pay the entire amount. The fee may run as high as four to five hundred dollars per month.

Suzanne's confusion over her own role in the home led her further into a troubled world. Her story emphasizes the need for shared responsibility in working through problems.

SUZANNE...

"I looked in the mirror."

Suzanne slouched into the court room. Her shirt was hanging out of her jeans. She reached back, tried to tuck it in, then shrugged. Her hair was disheveled. Her tennis shoes were dirty, one tie shorter than the other. Her tight fitting shirt revealed her well-developed figure. As she tucked the shirt in, she obviously tucked it in in such a way that it would be more revealing.

"Sit here," directed her probation officer as he held the chair for her.

"Here?" she asked as she turned to smile at the officer.

"Yes," he replied. "Suzy, be sure now to stand when the judge enters," the probation officer reminded her. "And don't get smart with him. He is not here to have you try to give him a snow job. He is here to say what happens. So play it cool. Be honest with him. Do you understand?"

"I am always honest," Suzy retorted, "it is just that you guys won't believe me. So, what can I do?"

"You can do your best," cautioned her probation officer, "and just don't smart off."

"Okay, I won't," promised Suzy as she slouched down in her chair.

Glancing to her left she noticed her attorney, appointed as guardian ad litem. She grinned at him.

"I hope you heard Mr. Long," said the attorney. "This judge does not like smart girls. Your folks are here. Do you want to speak with them?"

"Naw," said Suzanne. She sat chewing bubble gum, making bubbles periodically.

"Suzy, I think you better leave off on the bubbles. The judge may walk in and that would look kind of funny, don't you think?" asked the probation officer.

Suzy shifted, "Boy, I can't do anything to please you guys ... okay, if you say so!" She settled down, continuing to chew her gum.

Suzanne's parents were seated directly behind her. They appeared to be concerned people. Middle-aged, appropriately groomed, like many parents who come into the court, they looked bewildered, not understanding why this should happen in their family, confused as to which step to take next, unable to reach their daughter, but determined someone would have to stop her before she destroyed herself.

Mr. and Mrs. Landrow were people of modest, but comfortable means. They were hard-working, dependable people. They had a family of five children, two older than Suzanne and two younger. Mrs. Landrow worked three days a week to supplement her husband's salary, but for the most part, her time was spent in caring for family needs. She did receive some help from the children in doing the housework, but she was there to give them the guidance they needed. Until Suzanne was arrested as a runaway, the family was not known to the court. Now they had filed a petition alleging their daughter was an incorrigible child and asking that the court assist them in seeking an appropriate adjustment for her, whether it be in their home or in the home of another.

Suzanne had been at the Hall for three weeks. During this time, she attended school and entered into the activities with the other children, but for some reason she always seemed to be around when there were problems. As a result, she had spent some time in detention. On one occasion, she defied a house parent who would not allow her to stay out of school for a day and spend the day in her dorm room. As a result, she spent some time in security. While there, she caused some commotion, yelling over the intercom for her probation officer and making a general nuisance of herself. Directives from those in authority seemed to be her clue to rebel. Everyone who had come into contact with her felt the pressure. As one house parent said, "You feel like you are near a keg of dynamite with the fuse lit, or about to step on eggs!" Needless to say, Suzanne had not done well at the Hall. She neglected her school work, claiming, as her excuse, that she did not understand the assignment. She hassled with the other young people, often provoking fights. It was no wonder the probation officer and the attorney were cautioning her, and appeared a little tense in anticipation of the judge's meeting her.

A discussion with Suzanne was kind of an earth-shaking experience. She seemed to delight in making some shocking remark, totally disagreeing with any statement made, and all but making fun of the one with whom she was in discussion. She indicated she did not like her home, her parents, or anything connected with them. She did not like her brothers and sister, and felt they were stupid. She characterized her parents as "freaks who don't know what is going on." Home was a place where she was deprived of any wish she had. True, she had enough food, and she had clothes to wear, but they were not the kind she wanted. She had her own room, but "the kids go in and take my things." She was given an allowance, but "it was not enough to do anything with." She was allowed to have friends in, but "they (meaning her parents) don't like them." She was allowed to go out, but "I have to be in so early what is the use" (early meaning ten on school nights, midnight on weekends!).

This was her third run from home. On the first occasion, she had been gone for about two weeks and decided to return home. She indicated she got "hungry and tired," and thought it best to return. She had gone to friends that time, and had not communicated with her parents. The police were looking for her. "They are bums ... they could never find me if I didn't want them to ...."

The second time Suzanne ran from home it was summer. She hitchhiked down the coast. "The beaches were real cool, and the guys the greatest!" She spent most of her time on the beaches. She had saved some of her allowance each week and had enough to provide some food. But as food and money gave out, she frankly admitted she got her food where she could and for whatever charge. She became a sexually delinquent girl, experimented with drugs, and on one occasion was involved in the theft of a car. She was waiting on the corner for the fellows who were in the car to return for her. They were holding up a service station, and were caught. Suzanne ran, and for some reason avoided the police. She returned to her beach routine and was not arrested. She was caught by the beach police stealing food — she had ordered, but did not have money to pay, and walked away. A near-by police officer arrested her. She dealt with him skillfully. She had met some frequent visitors to the beach, and had been in their home on occasion. She told the officers she was from "around here" and the officer agreed to take her home rather than press charges. He took her to the home of her "friends" who went along with the situation, and she was released after the officer was given the money for the food. Her friends told her not to pull that again and she never saw them after that. The police began to watch her and she became apprehensive. She hitchhiked home. Her parents brought her to the Hall on that occasion. She remained for a few days and on the promise of "shaping up" was released.

Things went from bad to worse. She became openly defiant of her parents. She admitted to them she smoked and enjoyed marijuana. They smelled liquor on her breath frequently when she came in. She never kept her curfew and she was becoming involved with many questionable people. Her parents were desperate. One day she overheard her mother making a call to the probation officer and she ran.

This run took Suzanne to another state, hitchhiking again. She hitched rides with men who would put her up for the night for personal favors. They fed her and bought her clothes. When they let her off, she hitched a ride with another, and so it went. At last, about a month later, she hitched a ride with a man who was different. He did buy her some food, he found out what he wanted to know about her, and then he called the police who met him at a restaurant and took her into custody. "The dirty bum ... I should have killed him. I should have known he was a creep!"

Suzanne was returned to the Hall. Her parents rallied around to attempt to work with her. She rejected them completely. "I don't want to see them. Keep them away."

During the three weeks that Suzanne had been in the Hall, she had been seen by the psychologist. His report indicated deep depression, feelings of rejection, and a very poor self-image. He stated in his report he felt Suzanne was her own worst enemy. She was convinced she was no good and set out to convince the world of this. She was doing a pretty good job! The sad part of it was that she seemed to be enjoying it. Everyone dreaded an encounter with her. Any approach usually turned into a confrontation. The psychologist said her rejection of her parents was due to deep-seated guilt feelings. He indicated Suzanne was in need of intensive professional help if she were to ever make an adequate adjustment.

According to the probation officer, any attempt to work with Suzanne was fruitless. She argued, denied, and if he pushed her, simply refused to talk. She hated the staff at the Hall and let them know it.

Suzanne's past school record was quite revealing. She had good ability. She had experienced much illness during the early years of elementary school and as a result was on homebound instruction. She was in the hospital for periods of time, and all in all, did not have the advantage of interaction with other children. During this time, she demanded a great deal of her mother's attention. Suzanne's two younger brothers were born when she was in the sixth and seventh grades. Up to that time, Suzanne had been the baby of the family, and indeed she was! It was no doubt a blow to her when the younger children had to be cared for and she had to share her mother. According to the record, trouble started at school about that time. The family requested and received the services of trained personnel in working with her at school. As Suzanne grew older, she refused to enter into these attempts to assist her. The problems increased and became more serious. Her parents often expressed the hope she would "grow out of it." Now there was a serious division between the parents and Suzanne and to bring them together looked almost hopeless. The parents seemed to have given up. Suzanne acted as though she could not care less!

"Please rise!"

"This court is now in session. You may be seated," directed the clerk as the judge took his seat. Reading the petition, the judge outlined the complaint of the parents who alleged their daughter was out of their control, that they were unable to keep her at home, that they feared for her safety, and feared she was totally destroying herself, and were requesting help from the court. They asked that she be ordered to participate with them in a program of counseling.

"What is your position in this matter?" asked the judge of the guardian.

"Suzanne admits the facts," replied the attorney.

"Mr. Long, give the background and your recommendation, please," requested the judge.

"Your Honor, I will not take the time to go through the complete summary, as I have presented it to the court, but by the way of summation I would like to inform the court that this is Suzanne's third runaway, and each time she becomes more seriously involved in self-destructive activities. In addition, Suzanne is angry with her parents, refuses to return home, and is completely uncooperative, not only with them, but with me also. I must admit I am at a loss as to how to work with her. She is, as the petition alleges, an incorrigible girl, but also, as the report indicates, a girl with deep-seated emotional needs. She needs professional help. Her parents are willing to work with her, to involve themselves in counseling in an effort to try to understand better how to work with her, but she refuses. I would recommend she return home. That is where she belongs. Her parents want her there. I believe she would benefit from that. But, Your Honor, she will not agree to this."

When the probation officer completed his report, the judge turned to the parents. "Mr. and Mrs. Landrow, how can we help here? It appears we have a problem."

"I agree, Your Honor," Mr. Landrow was speaking, "and I want you to know we are anxious to help, but we don't know how. Suzanne refuses to speak with us. She says she will not return home. We are willing to have counseling help. We don't want her to hurt herself, but she seems determined. I guess we are hoping you can help us." Mr. Landrow's voice gave evidence of the concern he felt.

"Well, Suzanne, what do you have to say?" asked the judge.

"I don't want to go home. I don't like it there. I don't care what you do, but I won't go home."

"You don't like yourself very well, do you Suzanne?" asked the judge.

"Sure I do. There is nothing wrong with me . . ." Suzanne hesitated.

"What do you see when you look in the mirror, Suzanne?" asked the judge. "Are you pleased with what you see?"

"What kind of question is that?" asked Suzanne. "That is kind of dumb . . . ."

"No, not really, Suzanne. You are hurting yourself and your parents. Right now," the judge continued, "I believe you all love one another, but I don't think you like one another very well. I want you to look in the mirror every morning, and I want you to do this until you can really say to yourself 'I like what I see.' It is only then that others will begin to like you, and you will be able to like others. Love differs from like. We love others despite their actions, but for a good, wholesome relationship to exist we have to like a person — even members of our own family, even ourselves. Does that sound strange to you?"

"It sounds dumb to me," answered Suzanne, "but I ain't going home."

Turning to the attorney, the judge asked, "What is your recommendation?"

"Your Honor, I do not feel Suzanne can go home now. I wish she could, and I hope in a very short time she will realize what she is doing to herself. But for now, I recommend she live in a group home."

"Suzanne, I notice you have not cooperated very well with the psychologist, the house parents, or the teachers, and that you have said you are going to run away from here, is that right?" asked the judge.

"You better believe it! I hate this stupid place!"

"You really are filled with hate, Suzanne," the judge commented. "You do not leave me much choice. We need to know more about you before we can decide what is best for you. You will not allow us that opportunity here. So I am going to send you to the diagnostic center for an evaluation. In about a month, if you cooperate, you will return here with their recommendation and I will decide what happens then. If you go over there and refuse to work with them, you will leave me no choice but to change the order to a full commitment, which will mean you will be the responsibility of the state, until they feel you are able to be released. You have backed yourself into a corner. The game-playing is over. We will not play it your way any longer. We can detain you as long as it takes. You will be free to make it as uncomfortable for yourself as you like. I feel your parents have tried. The only thing I can find wrong is that they did not turn you across their knees and apply a little love on the back-side when you were younger. You are a spoiled, incorrigible child, and I think you know it. You seem to get pleasure from making others unhappy. Now, I refuse to let you do that any longer. You need professional help, I am sure. When you make up your mind you want to cooperate and conduct yourself like a lady, I am sure I will know. Until that time, I am committing you for a diagnostic evaluation. I wish you well, but that will be of little value unless you cooperate."

The judge rose. Everyone stood. He started to leave the court room.

"You know what you are," Suzanne yelled at him.

He turned, "What?"

"Never mind. You are too dumb to understand."

The judge returned to his seat.

"Sit down, young lady," he directed.

To the surprise of all, she sat.

"Now, stand!" She rose.

The judge turned to the probation officer. "Place her in detention until she can be taken from this facility. If she gives any one any more trouble, I want to be notified immediately. Mr. and Mrs. Landrow, I want to speak with you for a moment."

The probation officer directed Suzanne out of the court room. This time there was no outburst. The judge spoke with the parents.

"Do you understand what I have done?" he asked.

They shook their heads indicating they did not.

"I am committing her for a diagnostic evaluation. She will be seen by social workers, psychologists, and psychiatrists, and be able to attend school while she is at the diagnostic center. I would keep her here for that, but she will not cooperate. I know she has problems, but somehow we have to break that strong will. We will never be able to help her if she will not help herself. We can't hold her in the Hall unless we lock her up, and I don't want to do that. You will be asked to be a part of the procedure while she is at the center and I know you will cooperate. In about thirty days, the review board will meet and prepare their recommendation. She will come back here for disposition of her case. Hopefully by that time she will be willing to work with us and she can return home. In the meantime, try to relax. She will be safe. At least she will not be out there some place, alone and perhaps in personal danger. I know this is difficult for you, but we can't back down now. Does this help any?"

"Yes, thank you, Your Honor. We appreciate your explanation very much," Mr. Landrow spoke for himself and his wife. "We will do everything we can to cooperate."

"I know you will. I appreciate that."

The judge left the court room. The hearing was over. The brokenhearted parents of a deeply-hurting incorrigible child walked out.

The month passed. Suzanne was before the court for disposition. She had settled down. During this month she had the opportunity to realize she would only prolong detention if she refused to cooperate. As she relaxed her defensiveness, she found she could actually work with people and that they were not against her. She began to see herself as a part of the family rather than caught between two older siblings and two younger siblings. There were smiles on the faces of the parents. Suzanne spoke briefly with them before the judge entered. She stood attentively as he took his seat.

"Well, Suzanne, your report looks good. Are you ready to tell me how you feel about all of this?" The judge waited for her response.

"I would like to try it at home ... " Suzanne looked down, hesitated for a moment, then looked up. "My mom and dad really put themselves out while I was at the center. They came to see me every time they could. I think I need some counseling help. I would like to try, if I can."

"Well, Suzanne, that seems to be the recommendation, so we will give it a try. Mr. Long has arranged for counseling help for you and your parents. I have an idea things will work out very well with your cooperation. They cannot do it alone, nor can you. They have always been willing to work at it, and now you are. So there is no reason why it shouldn't work out. Now, there will be some discouragement, but don't let that throw you. Just pick yourself up by the boot straps and try again. Home is where you belong, not on the streets. You have a good life ahead of you. You are a capable, attractive girl, and you are surrounded by people who care. Good luck to you."

The judge rose to go. Everyone stood.

"Your Honor," Suzanne hesitated, "I looked in the mirror this morning."

The judge smiled. "What did you see?" he asked.

"I liked what I saw," she said.

"Good!" replied the judge. "So do I like what I see now."

As the judge left the court room, Suzanne joined her parents. There was a way to go, but they were on their way and with a good start. The love was there. It only needed the opportunity to prove itself.

Chapter 10

Another classification of dependent is the battered and abused child. In this land of America, with all of its progress and prosperity and opportunity, why the continued increase in the number of battered and abused children? Pick up any periodical article relating to this subject. It is frightening! Thousands and thousands of children are being reported each year by members of the medical profession, school staff, police, and others.

But why? The tempted abuser is offered so much social service assistance in today's society. Family counseling, economic counseling, mental health care, and medical service are all available.

And yet, I have seen little three and four year olds, tongue blistered by a cigarette; I have seen little ones with hands and arms burned from being placed under the faucet with water turned on to the hottest temperature, with bottoms burned from being placed on a hot stove. I have seen tiny tots, barely able to walk, sometimes still in the crib, with broken bones caused by being bounced against a wall, arms pulled and jerked, or legs hit with some object. I have seen eyes swollen shut from being struck with a fist, broken, bruised skin criss-crossed by welts from the face down to the feet! I have known of warrants signed for the arrest of some adult for the death of an infant or small child following severe blows in the stomach area, the head, or other parts of the body!

Who commits such heinous acts? Parents! Or parent! Or the boy friend of the mother or the girl friend of dad!

What possible reasons can be given for committing such acts? None that could ever be valid!

Investigations reveal that children are abused because they cry too long, because they will not go to sleep, because they wet their diapers or pants, because they will not eat, because they do not obey at the first command! They are abused because some weak, self-willed adult loses his temper.

Some parents admit that the child was not wanted, or perhaps was not the desired sex. Other rationalizations are that the child is deformed or funny-looking, or is a reminder of another person, or is retarded. Family problems such as economics, alcoholism, or family discord may be presented as the reason. The child may be characterized as difficult to manage, or as being different from other children — apathetic, submissive, never crying.

Some authorities claim that child abusers were themselves victims of abuse. This may be true, but if so, they should have learned lessons that would prohibit such a pattern of behavior. It has also been suggested that the abuser has a poor self image, has ambivalent feelings toward parents, toward discipline, toward self and others. Whatever the reason, it may be an explanation, but is there ever an excuse?

Children are often battered and abused physically for long periods of time before detection. It is only when the parent fears severe injury and takes the child for medical care that the situation is discovered. By that time it may be too late for protection of the child within the family unit. The court may need to separate the child from the home.

National concern over the ever increasing number of reported and unreported cases of battered and abused children is growing. The laws of the nation speak to this concern. There is a penalty for not reporting suspected cases of battering and abuse, and there is immunity for the person reporting. Under a statute of protection, the abused child is being discovered and reported more often. In most states, responsibility for investigating reported cases is in the hands of the Children's Protective Services.

While it is true that physical, medical, educational, moral, and emotional *neglect* are very difficult to deal with in the adjudication of dependency, it is absolutely vital that physical, sexual, emotional, and drug *abuse* be dealt with!

Physical Abuse

Physical abuse is non-accidental. It may or may not cause visible damage. It is usually repetitive. It is often fatal!

I have observed little children following such abuse. Helpless, totally dependent, reaching out little arms of love to the one who beat them! These children love their parents. Even though in pain, they are forgiving. Even though the cruel treatment has continued for some time, the child wants that person he calls mom or dad. With little arms lifted in love and faith, he offers himself to that person. For what? To be battered and abused again!

Do I sound bitter ... disgusted ... angry? I am! You come with me for a visit with little Brenda. She is being wheeled into the court room, her little leg stretched forward in a cast that goes up to the hip. Her tiny arm is also in a cast. On her beautiful face are signs of deep bruises. Her blond curls surround a baby face from which two deep blue eyes look hurt and bewildered. Seated in the court room is the man who caused this. The investigation revealed that the working mother is shacking up with a husky twenty four year old who weighs close to two hundred pounds. He sits comfortably, convinced he has done no wrong. Little Brenda reaches toward her mother. The young woman attempts to comfort her.

The story is told. Neighbors heard sounds coming from the apartment which indicated a child was being thrown against the wall. Screams would penetrate the air. Then silence. After several days, the neighbors finally called the police. Brenda had almost been killed that night. The young man had been acting as sitter while the mother was at work. He had grown angry when Brenda would not go to sleep and interrupted his TV watching. Now he was sitting in court, trying to reason with the judge!

"Animals treat their young better than this! Your actions are contemptible! You had better be thankful you will not appear before me in court! You are some man to pit your strength against this child!"

Let's view another court scene. A well-groomed young couple enters the room. The young man is perhaps in his early twenties, the young lady is no older than late teens. She is carrying little three month old Jon. Mother holds the baby fondly. Looking at him lovingly, she speaks softly to him. Following a battering, his frightened parents had taken him to the hospital. The child had been hospitalized with a broken femur and head injury. The abuse was reported, and Jon was placed in an interim foster home pending the court hearing.

"I have had similar cases," said the judge. "The difference in one was that the charge against the father was homicide. This is serious business! I just hope you recognize it as such. If you don't, I will see you again. My main concern is for your child. We will provide protection and care for him until you can get yourselves straightened out."

As little Jon was handed over by the mother to the custody of the court, she leaned down and kissed the child. There was no doubt but that she was touched by having to give him up. But this was not the fault of the child. Had such loving care been afforded the child during daily routine living, this scene never would have been viewed by those of us in the court room.

Pictures are often shown in court of children who have been whipped with belts, light cords, or perhaps sticks until there is not a space left on the little body that is not damaged! Haunting eyes stare from sad, emaciated faces. Public school staff are often the first to discover this abuse. Children confide in those they trust! The appropriate agency is called. When the evidence is sufficient, the case is referred to the court. Possibly for the first time in many months, a child may go to sleep that night feeling safe, but missing his mommie and daddy. Battered and abused victims are usually pre-school children, or if they are in school, they are elementary school age. The small group of abused older children are usually self-referrals. They show the body marks from a beating. They ask for and are granted protective custody. These children file their own petitions. They ask for placement out of the home. Parents do not often challenge this.

Sexual Abuse

Sexually abused children are equally as heartbreaking. Victims suffer deep psychological damage and often physical damage as well. Older female children are usually the victims of such abuse, but this is not always so. Cases have been referred to court involving entire families — father against daughters, mothers and sons, even grandparents. In one case heard, the father was "training" the older boys to be men by demonstrations with the younger girls — sisters of the boys! A stepfather is often attracted to a teenage stepdaughter. He shows his so-called affection by sexual advances. If rejected, he may use other means of pursuit — he may threaten, or he may buy her gifts which please her. Eventually one of two things happens. Either the wife finds out and takes action or the girl becomes angry or guilt-ridden and turns him in. One stepfather impregnated his ten year old stepdaughter. She aborted. An investigation ensued. In the court hearing the mother of the child told the court "he has been a good father to her — except for this one instance!" The man was charged. The child was found to be dependent and placed out of the home.

It is not unusual for a woman to throw a wall of protection around her husband in these cases. She willingly states in court she does not believe the child. She admits she had been told of the circumstances existing but did nothing about it. Investigation will sometimes reveal that sexual abuse has gone on for several years. The girl will finally find the courage to tell her mother. Mother's reaction is very important. If she refutes the claim, the child may continue in the situation until she finds the courage to seek outside help. If the mother is supportive, together they do so. There have been instances when a married daughter comes to the court seeking help for younger sisters remaining in the home who are being subjected to the same treatment she previously received.

Not all mothers, of course, are supportive of husbands involved in sexual abuse of their daughters. One such mother reported to the court she had moved her things out of the home, reported him to the police, was glad he was arrested, and had a restraining order placed on the man following his release on bail. Each of her three daughters had been subjected to sexual abuse by their father when they reached a certain age. Eventually, they had confided in one another and had come to the court for help. These girls were beautiful, excellent students, and well liked by peers and adults. They were placed under the protective care of their mother.

Not all sexually abused girls are older children. Michelle was about two years old when I first met her. She was a little dumplin'. Toddling around in the nursery of the detention facility, she was consumed by fear of men. She had been sexually assaulted by her mother's boy friend. Because of the physical damage to her little body, she had spent many days in the hospital. She carried with her such a memory of the attack and the pain suffered that she cried and screamed if a man came near her. She found comfort in the arms of one of the women house parents, and would cling to this lady, who would spend hours holding, loving, and rocking her. In the evenings I would frequently visit the children in the nursery. On this particular warm evening my husband went with me to see the children. As we walked toward the door, little Michelle toddled out to meet us. She was smiling, then laughing. She went directly to my husband. Standing before him, she lifted up her chubby little arms for him to take her. He gathered her up! She put her little arms around him! He was the first man she had responded to. Needless to say, our tears flowed. The parent was deprived of this beautiful child. I often wonder whether she has been able to forget the horrible experience she was subjected to.

There are many little Michelles and older girls who have gone through similar experiences. Many of these cases are never reported. Family and relatives keep things like this quiet. Incest is an ugly word. It carries with it a social stigma. Families know what the reaction of society will be. Even the child herself may begin to feel guilty and a part of a very dirty experience. It is only when she is emotionally able to handle such an experience that she realizes she must do something about it.

There is another side of sexual abuse that should be mentioned here. This is the case of the teenage girl who becomes angry with her mother or father, or stepfather, and comes to the court with the charge that he has forced himself on her. When the investigation proves no facts, eventually the girl breaks down and admits her lie, or some skilled probation officer, or even the judge, may see through it all.

"She was angry with us," said one mother. "She wanted us to allow her to go out, stay out as late as she pleased, and go with whomever she pleased. We refused. After all, she is only thirteen!"

In this hearing, the judge admonished the girl. "You should be ashamed of yourself. You come in here and tell a bunch of lies. You try to set someone up and all because you are a selfish, spoiled brat! What you need is to be taken to the woodshed. I hope you some day understand what you have done. I would not blame your parents if they ask me to send you somewhere else to live."

"We want her home," stated the father. "She is just a kid. She has picked up a lot of street talk. The best way to keep her away from that is to keep her off the street. I think we can manage. I would like to take her home."

Emotional Abuse

Not only physical and sexual, but emotional abuse is becoming more and more of major concern. Psychological evaluations reveal the emotional turmoil suffered by children from homes where they are dealt with in a punitive way, where there is hostility between members of the family, where they experience verbal abuse, where parents are always critical, and where they can never experience success. In some homes children's loyalties are constantly torn between parents, or the children live in constant fear of being sent from the home or perhaps having a parent leave the home. These too are emotionally damaging experiences. Children often begin to act out as a result of such treatment. Or, they may withdraw. Often much damage is done before the situation is discovered.

Drug Abuse

In recent years another form of abuse — drug abuse — has been under a great deal of discussion. Children are sedated to quiet them. The expectant mother is sometimes a drug user while carrying the child. Cases have been investigated where parents have "shared" their liquor and controlled substances with children.

Child abuse is against the law, and the law should be upheld. But laws do not protect children. They only allow for the protection of children. Ginger's story testifies to the heartache and difficult decision confronting the battered child.

GINGER ..

"No use for child beaters."

The sunlight seemed to be playing games with Ginger's hair. The beams danced through the open drapery and seemed to delight in highlighting the beautiful auburn hair of the silently weeping sixteen year old. It was a warm, sunny day — the kind of day that seemed to be made especially for young people to look expectantly to a beautiful world for better days filled with excitement. It was a lazy, carefree day, one in which trouble should be far removed, leaving only the sunlight and the blue skies to reflect youthful anticipation. The reality of the court room scene, the sobs of the beautiful girl, mocked the serenity of the day.

As Ginger's sobs became audible the probation officer went to her side. She placed her arm around Ginger's shoulder and attempted to comfort her. "You must get hold of yourself. This is not going to help you, or me, when His Honor comes in. Now, you know what we have talked about. You know things are going to be all right. Please, will you trust me? Do you want a drink?"

Ginger shook her head no. She leaned against the probation officer. "Why did it have to come to this? Why? Why?"

"Ginger, you have done the right thing. Please try to relax. I know it is difficult, but sometimes we have to do things that are hard in order to make things right," the probation officer continued to comfort the girl. At last Ginger gained composure and straightened herself in her chair. She looked at her probation officer and rewarded her with a sad smile.

Throughout this, the guardian ad litem for Ginger sat with a determined expression, his presence seeming to blend steel with the gentle, fragile appearance of Ginger. His expression left little doubt that he was her advocate and would stand in her stead, defying any provocation which might cast a shadow of blame in her direction.

Ginger turned toward him. "Thank you for your help ... and your kindness," she said.

"That's all right. Everything will be okay," the guardian assured her. It was evident that he was emotionally upset by Ginger's distress and though he wanted to comfort her, he very simply stated, "It won't take too long ... the judge will be in shortly." With that he left the court room abruptly, perhaps to get a drink, perhaps to walk off some of his own tension. He was gone for a few moments, returning to seat himself at Ginger's side and to busy himself with the papers on his desk.

The moments seemed to drag, but allowed time for mental review of the record. Ginger had referred herself to the juvenile court because her home situation had become unbearable. She feared for her younger brother and three sisters, and while she did not enter them with herself for protective custody and shelter care, she did discuss her concern with the intake officer with the result that the younger children had been picked up on a warrant and placed in interim foster care pending the court disposition.

Ginger's story was filled with heartache. Her father was an alcoholic who repeatedly beat her mother and the children. When she entered herself at the Hall, Ginger carried on her body the results of a severe beating — belt marks across her back, down her legs, and across her face. In addition to the fresh evidence of a beating were signs of previous attacks — the yellow and black bruises and the scars where the flesh had been cut deeply on one occasion when she had been beaten with a light cord.

In giving an account to the court, Ginger said that because she feared for her mother's safety, she was reluctant to come to the court. She was afraid her father would seek revenge, blame her mother, and take out on her his wrath toward Ginger. She stated the smaller children had received severe beatings. Her younger sister was bedridden and had been for a week because of a severe beating. On this occasion, Ginger said, the child's eyes were closed from being hit in the face. Her face was swollen and discolored, and she ran a temperature for almost the full week because of the ordeal. Her mother was afraid to take the child to a doctor, knowing full well this would have to be reported. She feared the retaliation of her drinking husband, not only for herself but for the children. One evening during this same week, the father, still drinking, went into the bedroom where her little sister was in bed. He grabbed her and threw her against the wall, yelling that he would kill her if she did not get out of the bed and stay out. Ginger said this was the only time she saw her mother defy him. Running to the child, who had passed out and was on the floor, the mother gathered her up, gently placed her on the bed, and turning to her husband said, "Don't touch her again ... I mean it!" Ginger said there must have been something about the mother's voice that made her father know she meant what she said. At that point her father turned, left the room, went to his bottle, slumped on the davenport, and was soon asleep.

During this same week the father came home very drunk and attacked Ginger, beating her severely with his belt because she did not move fast enough to please him. He had demanded something to eat. Ginger began to dish up his food. He became angry and beat her. In attempting to avoid the blows, Ginger received several lashes across her face with the belt. The spots were still visible a week later. Her back was covered with belt lashes which had cut over healing lashes that had been previously administered. On this occasion Ginger began to really fear for her life. Her father had knocked her down and was savagely attacking her, yelling, "I will kill you. I will kill all of you ... you are no good. You are just like your mother ... disobey me, will you?" Ginger had fled the home, but rather than call for police protection she came to the Hall and asked to be entered for shelter care and protective custody.

Ginger looked back at former times. She said that she could not remember the time her father did not drink. He had not always been an excessive drinker, but as time went by he became more and more dependent on the bottle. He had been a professional man when she was a small child, but drink caused him to lose out and he drifted from job to job, becoming more and more dependent on alcohol. Ginger indicated she could recall her mother begging him to get professional help for the problem and that for a time he did receive counseling, but then he took the next drink and from there he continued to go down hill. The family began to suffer financial stress. The home was sold, a less expensive one purchased. The payments could not be made on that and it was sold. Soon the family resorted to rentals, each one becoming less suitable as they were forced to move because of failure to pay the rent. Now the home was most inadequate. Located in a depressed area of the city, it offered little comfort to the mother and children. Her father could not care less. He drifted from job to job until now the family was receiving public assistance and the little money received was first spent on liquor. There were days, declared Ginger, when there was little to eat, and the mother encouraged the children to accept any invitation from a friend that might be offered. The mother began to do housework for friends of acquaintances in an attempt to supplement. One day her husband came drunk to the home where she was working. He was verbally abusive to the homeowners and marginally physically abusive to his wife. He accused her of trying to humiliate him by being a domestic and ordered her home. Ginger said when they returned home her mother was beaten severely and ordered never to work as a domestic again. Since that time her mother had been doing ironing in her own home when the father was out, hiding it when he returned in order to avoid open conflict.

According to Ginger, her father seemed possessed and compelled to beat them when he reached a certain point. Even when not drunk, he was never kind or gentle with them. He was never remorseful even if he happened to observe the marks on their bodies when he was sober. His only comment was, "You brought it on yourself." This had gone on for years. Ginger said it was because of fear for their lives that she did not come to the Hall before this.

When Ginger entered herself at the Hall, the protective service unit was sent to the home to investigate. The investigating officer confirmed Ginger's report. The home was in disarray. After Ginger had left the house, her father had broken much of the furniture, and had beaten two of the smaller children. The mother was confused and bewildered. She did not know which way to turn. She had no relatives. She feared what might happen if she went to the police. She was exhausted, emotionally and physically. She pleaded for her children to be cared for, indicating she would remain in the home and take whatever punishment her husband administered. Her concern was for her children. There was little food in the home. The clothing of the children, while clean, was limited. It was a pathetic situation.

A warrant was served, and the children were placed in interim foster care. The mother was provided temporary shelter which would enable her to feel more safe. The father was arrested and charged with child abuse. He was now out on bail pending trial. He had been served a summons to appear at this hearing. This, no doubt, was what was upsetting Ginger. She did not know what might possibly happen if he should appear in court drunk. She was fully aware of what the possibilities might be.

The door of the court opened and two deputies appeared. They seated themselves in strategic locations in the court room. It was obvious the probation officer and guardian had prepared for any situation which might develop. Somehow, the appearance of two officers seemed to cloak the court room with a blanket of safety. They were well trained and prepared to meet any crisis and deal with it accordingly. It would be a foolish person who would challenge either of them.

Shortly after the officers seated themselves, Ginger's mother was brought into the court room, appearing nervous and distraught. She stood momentarily, not knowing what was expected of her. The probation officer went to her and directed her to Ginger's side. The mother leaned down and kissed her daughter. "Don't worry," she whispered "you did the right thing. I wish I had your courage." Ginger clung to her mother and for a moment there was only mother and daughter. The mother took her seat behind Ginger.

The door opened again. Ginger's father entered, escorted in by one of the male probation officers. Following him were two more male probation officers. Here was the wife and child beater. The professional man who had succumbed to drink. Behind the shadow-rimmed eyes, the graying hair and the drawn, shrunken, emaciated features, one could visualize what he might have been. He stood over six feet tall and gave the appearance that he could have presented himself very well in the professional world. With a little imagination, it was easy to picture him in a business suit, holding a responsible position. Had he not been so thin and drawn, he would have been a handsome man. He paused briefly, and then sat in the seat to which he was directed. The room was silent. No one moved.

Suddenly Ginger was on her feet. She turned toward her father. The guardian rose. "It is all right," said Ginger. She motioned the attorney away, and moved toward her father. Leaning before him she said, "I am sorry. I had to do what I did. I hope you understand. We do love you. But I could not go on this way. I could not stand to see you hurt mom and the kids any longer. You are hurting yourself, too. Won't you get some help? Please!"

Her father looked at her, his face expressionless, defeated. Observing him, one could not help but wish that he would break completely and reach out to his daughter as a sign he was able to understand his need. He did not speak. Suddenly Ginger rose and returned to her seat. She hung her head. The sunbeams began to play games with her auburn hair again. The room was silent.

"Please rise!"

The court clerk was entering the court room. The judge followed. On the clerk's directive, everyone took his seat. His Honor was now in control.

Surveying the room with a sweeping glance, the judge rested his eyes on the father, then shifted to the mother. Neither returned his look. At last he rested his eyes on Ginger. She looked at him confidently and as they communicated momentarily in this way, Ginger seemed to relax.

The judge read the petition. It alleged that Ginger, her three sisters and her brother were dependent children because of the severe beatings they had suffered at the hands of their father and because of the overall conditions of the home, the father being an alcoholic, the mother financially unable to care for them without assistance from the state. The petition further requested that the children not be returned to the mother unless a restraining order was placed on the father pending his court hearing. He was not to be allowed near the home where the children were to reside, nor was he to be allowed to visit with them until visitation arrangements were approved by the court. The situation was such, according to the petition, that the court should review the matter within ninety days. At that time, the disposition of the father's pending court hearing, what he had done to rehabilitate himself, the action taken by the mother to secure the children's future, and the feelings of the children themselves would be reviewed. The petition requested that the children be made temporary wards of the court and returned to the mother's physical custody under specific conditions and supervision of the court. The petition was filed and signed by the probation officer and a copy of the findings of the investigating officers and staff from Children's Protective Services was a part of the record.

"I have been on this bench a long time," began the judge. "I have heard hundreds of cases, both in this court and in superior court. This is one of the worst I have ever encountered." Turning to the guardian he said, "Do you have any comments to make at this time?"

"Your Honor," said the attorney, "I agree with the statement you have just made. The record speaks for itself. I will not put Ginger through any more by verbally expressing my feelings regarding so many aspects of the case. Ginger wants to return to her mother. I want to be sure that the mother will have the courage to care for the children as she should. Otherwise, my recommendation is for foster care for all of them. The smaller children are not in the court room. They are available for the court to speak with if you so desire."

The judge turned to the probation officer. "Would you care to comment on further facts of the case?" he asked.

"Your Honor," said the probation officer, "these children deserve a chance — a chance to live. I have been constantly amazed that they have been able to survive through the years with all they have had to bear. I too am concerned about their safety. I want the assurance that the mother is capable of caring for them, enforcing the order of the court, and I want to be sure she will report any violation on the part of her husband to the proper authorities. If Your Honor is satisfied that the return of the children to their mother is appropriate, I would have no objections."

The judge addressed the attorney and the probation officer with the same comments: "Be assured that these children will not be returned to their mother's home unless this court is satisfied they will be safe. Be assured, also, that the home will be supervised by someone delegated by this court." Turning to the mother, the judge commented, "Mrs. Adams, whether you think so or not, you share in this tragedy that is before me.

I don't know whether you realize it, but as the mother of these children you are charged with their safety. I do not understand why you let this go on. I would like to hear from you."

"Please, Your Honor," Ginger pleaded. "She did try ... she has been hurt so much ... please!"

"Ginger," said the judge, "I want you to know, I do understand your feelings. I know you have gone through a great deal. But you cannot, under any circumstances, assume the responsibilities of your mother or of your father in this case. Would you like to be excused while I hear from them?"

"No," whispered Ginger. As she lowered her head, the tears streamed down her cheeks.

"Your Honor," began Mrs. Adams, "I know I was wrong. I have no excuse. I guess I wanted so badly for my husband to come to his senses and to realize we all love him and that he should get some help. The children and I talked about this frequently. We lived in hopes of his getting cured. There used to be better days ... he was a bright man. He wouldn't have to be this way ...." Her voice trailed off. "He is destroying all of us, and I almost let him kill my children. During these past two weeks I have thought a great deal. I know now my children must come first. I am separating from him until he can get the help he needs. If he cares enough for us and for himself, he will do that. I will ask for the restraining order, and if he does come around the house I will report him. I don't want to hurt him, but I hope the court does whatever is necessary to make him get some help."

The judge sat, waiting as though he was aware the mother had not completed what she had to say. Finally she continued, "I want my daughter to know I am proud of what she did. I wish I had been as strong as she has been. I have failed the children, too, but if you will allow me the chance I will take good care of them. I want my home to be supervised, and I will be willing to work to support my children. I have some training. Both my husband and I went to college. We have a good education, but you wouldn't think so the way things have been. I love my children, Your Honor. I want them to come home. I promise I will take good care of them." Ginger was openly sobbing now. Her mother had completed her remarks to the court. She put her hands over her face and she, too, sobbed. Both mother and daughter regained composure within a few seconds and raised their heads to hear the judge's next comments.

"Mr. Adams." There was a pause. The judge's voice was stern. He seemed to be searching for the appropriate words. "I have some things to say to you. I am not going to ask you what you are going to do. I don't even want to hear from you. There is absolutely no answer that is acceptable for what you have done. I just want you to know that it doesn't take much of a man to stoop so low as to beat children. Such action as you have demonstrated can only mean one of two things. Either you are just a mean person, or you are a sick man. You better get your thinking together and figure out which one it is. Personally, the title 'man' is not appropriate in this case. A real man never behaves in this way. Neither does a real father. If your children never speak to you again, you will get what you deserve. What your wife does about you is up to her. But you may be sure as long as these children are wards of the court they will be protected from the likes of you. And if you so much as go near them, much less touch them, I will have you thrown in jail and you won't see sunlight for a long time. I have no use for child beaters! You are just fortunate you will not be coming before me for your hearing. I would show no mercy." Mr. Adams was visibly shaken by the judge's remarks. He did not attempt to speak.

"Ginger, look at me. I want to say some things to you," spoke the judge. "You have done the right thing. It is not your fault that your home is not together ... you did not have a home the way things were. You acted responsibly in helping the younger children by coming to the Hall. I want you to remember that. I am going to let you go with your mother. Remember, you are not to be the mother of this family, because she is. If she does not assume that role, you children will be placed in foster care. We cannot stand by and let you be beaten and abused this way. Can you understand me?"

"Yes, I do understand," answered Ginger. "I guess I just wish we could have a home and be like other people. It just seems terrible that something like liquor could keep us from living like other kids. I do hope my dad will get some help. I know my mom will do what you say. I think they really do love us. Maybe some day things can be different."

"I hope so," said the judge. "But in the meantime, I want this home closely supervised, and if there is even an inkling that things are falling apart, I want action immediately. Is that understood?" The probation officer, the guardian ad litem, and Children's Protective Service workers nodded their agreement.

The judge rose to leave the court room. The hearing was over. Ginger went to her mother. They embraced and with arms around each other they turned toward Ginger's father. He looked at them, and without a word turned and walked out of the court room.

As I spoke with the mother periodically through several months, it was evident she had still not been able to really think through what had happened. She did as the court ordered, and she cared for her children well. Once again they were attending their church. Although the scars will remain through a lifetime, they were at last able to sit at the dinner table, to chat together, to laugh and plan together. The children continued to do well in school. Mrs. Adams did get a job and was able to support herself and the children comfortably.

"Sometimes," she said, "I miss him. I often wonder what happened to him. I think he must have just gone away. He never did bother us again, never came around. I would like to feel he loved us enough that he did what he thought was best. I do hope he did get the help he needed. He really was a good man, but alcohol destroyed him ... and almost destroyed us."

Part Three

View of the Problem and Solutions

Chapter 11:

Scope of the Problem

Lucy looked cute in her blue jeans and checkered shirt. She was small, almost fragile in appearance, a deceptive appearance according to her probation officer. "She reminds me of Ado Annie in Oklahoma, Your Honor. She has no moral standards. She frankly admits she gets pleasure out of her so-called love affairs. I have talked with her, and talked with her. It just doesn't make sense. Her parents can be of no help. They too are at a loss to understand her. They have loved, paddled, threatened, taken her to a psychiatrist, sent her to private school — the whole works. Everything has failed. They leave her five minutes and she has a fellow in. She is in bed with him, or on the couch, or on the floor — it makes no difference where. Her parents do not feel they can be of any assistance to her. They are asking the court to place her where she can have twenty-four hour a day supervision and where someone can possibly get to the bottom of this. When I asked Lucy, 'Don't you think this kind of behavior is wrong?', she answered, 'No, I don't. I like it. I'll keep doing it.' That is where we are now."

Chad's appearance gave one the impression of the All American Boy. He was well-built and well-groomed, and presented himself in a most courteous manner. He was before the court for armed robbery. Chad's parents told the court he was "quiet and obedient at home ... never gave us one bit of trouble ... we had no idea this was going on." Chad told his probation officer he thought he should begin planning his future, and since he had no money and no job, he tried to think of the best way to work this out. He felt he could steal articles, sell them, and bank the money without his parents' knowledge. He felt it unfair to ask his parents to supply the money necessary for the college education he desired. He was a good student and of college material. Burglarizing homes proved to be remunerative to begin with. As time passed, Chad wanted bigger and better things. He felt these could be acquired by going into businesses after hours. This proved successful for a period of time. Chad had a buyer for the merchandise. He was building up quite a bank account. Then he decided taking money would be an easier way. He bought himself a gun. "I wouldn't steal one." He attempted to hold up a service station. Something went wrong. He ran. For a time he went back to stealing merchandise. The gain was slow. School would soon be out. He needed more money for a car and college tuition, and perhaps a nice vacation before beginning college. He thought of armed robbery again, and tried it. This time he was knocked in the head by the owner of the service station as he held a gun on the attendant. He was arrested and charged with an alleged delinquent act. "Your plans will be postponed for quite awhile, I'm afraid," said the judge. "This kind of action never takes you to higher ground and greater opportunities. It only takes you in one direction and that is down! It is always a long road back."

Rich had stolen a car when he left the institution without permission. He drove to his home town and picked up his buddies. The mother of one of his friends became suspicious and called the police. A wild chase took place. For miles the police car pursued the car driven by the juvenile. One of the boys in the car had a gun. He threw it out of the car moments before the accident occurred. Police in two counties attempted to stop the car before it careened into a metal fence and came to a halt. No one was seriously injured, though all could have been killed. Rich's record indicated violations of the law since age thirteen. He was now sixteen. His future seemed to be pretty well settled as he faced the judge. "You must like jail. You are doing your best to spend the rest of your life there."

There are many Lucys and Chads and Richs appearing before the juvenile courts throughout the country today. Their violations are varied. Their motivations appear to be the same — self-gratification.

Juvenile delinquency is on the increase nationally. A discussion at any level indicates a growing concern and a sense of urgency in finding some deterrent. Community effort is being extended through agencies and individuals with the hope that a solution to the problem will soon be found.

In considering the scope of the problem, statistics present some interesting insights. While worthy of consideration, caution should be exercised in interpreting these facts. For various reasons statistics may not be the final authority in establishing an accurate view of the problem.

One major reason is that not all delinquent acts are reported, often for fear of reprisal or because "it is not worth the hassle." The offended person would prefer to take the loss. A second reason statistics may not present an accurate picture is that all young people arrested are referred to juvenile court. Other agencies within the juvenile system may work with the individual, or the arresting officer may elect to take the young offender home and allow his parents to work through the problem, or he may refer him to another police agency. There are options available, depending on the seriousness of the act and the attitude of the young person. Third, many acts of delinquency are committed for which there is no suspect. Such acts may appear insignificant, and police officers may not put forth maximum effort in attempting to establish identity of the person or persons involved, but this does not change the classification of the act. Finally, statistical facts should be interpreted in relation to the kind of information that is being sought and what the facts represent — individuals or numbers of violations?

Uniform Crime Reports for the United States, issued by Clarence M. Kelley, Director of the Federal Bureau of Investigation for the year 1975, makes some interesting observations which will be helpful in considering the scope of juvenile delinquency.

This report points out the fact that the total number of criminal acts that occur is unknown. Those reported to law enforcement agencies provide the first means of a count. Tabulations used in this report indicate the "probable extent, fluctuation, the distribution of crime in the United States as a whole."[1] One measure used is the Crime Index which consists of seven important offenses: murder/non-negligent manslaughter; forcible rape; robbery; aggravated assault; burglary/breaking or entering; larceny/theft; and motor vehicle theft. Statistical data relating to youth under eighteen years of age are included.[2]

According to the FBI report, there were an estimated 20,510 murders committed in the United States in 1975, a decrease of one percent from 1974. Ten percent of all persons arrested for murder were under eighteen years of age. Of all individuals processed for murder, nine percent were juveniles whose cases were referred to juvenile jurisdiction. There was, according to the report, a 28 percent increase in the number of persons under age eighteen arrested for murder during the period 1970–1975.[3]

Aggravated assaults increased during 1975. The volume increased six percent over 1974 and 45 percent over 1970. Arrests for aggravated assault increased 38 percent over 1970. Arrests for persons under eighteen years of age have increased 57 percent since 1970. Aggravated assault is defined as "an unlawful attack by one person upon another person for the purpose of inflicting severe bodily injury, usually accompanied by the use of a weapon or other means likely to produce death or serious bodily harm."[4]

Forcible rape is defined in the FBI report as "carnal knowledge of a female through the use of force or threat of force." The volume of forcible rape offenses increased one percent over 1973, and 48 percent over 1970. The arrests of persons under eighteen years of age increased by four percent over 1974. The greatest concentration of arrests made was in the sixteen to twenty-four years age bracket. Fifty-eight percent of all arrests made during the year were of persons under the age of 25. Figures for the years 1970–1975 show an increase of nineteen percent in arrests of persons under eighteen years of age.[5] Juvenile referrals amounted to 21 percent of the persons processed on forcible rape charges in 1975.

Robbery is a crime that takes place in the presence of the victim. By use of force or threat, property or an article of value is taken. There was a five percent increase in reported robberies during 1975 over 1974, with a 33 percent increase over 1970. Arrests of persons under age eighteen accounted for 34 percent of the 1975 total. This was an eleven percent increase over 1974. Thirty-seven percent of all people processed for robbery were juveniles whose cases were referred to the juvenile court.[6]

Burglary is defined as "unlawful entry with the intent to commit a felony or theft." Force may or may not be used. Burglary increased six percent over 1974 and 41 percent over 1970. Total arrests for burglary in 1975 increased by seven percent over 1974. Arrests of persons under eighteen years of age increased six percent and accounted for 53 percent of all arrests for this crime.[7] Fifty-seven percent of all persons processed for burglary in 1975 were juveniles.

The FBI report defines larceny/theft as "the unlawful taking or stealing of property or articles without the use of force, violence or fraud." Such crimes as shop-lifting, purse-snatching, thefts from motor vehicles, or motor vehicle parts, and pocket picking are included. For the period 1970–75 there was an increase of 35 percent in crimes reported in this category. There was an increase of fourteen percent in 1975 as compared to 1974. Arrests increased eight percent over the same period. Forty-five percent of these arrests were of persons under age eighteen. Forty percent of those processed for this crime in 1975 were referred to juvenile jurisdiction.[8]

There was a two percent increase nationally in 1975 over 1974 of vehicles reported stolen. Since 1970 there has been an eight percent increase in this crime. Fifty-five percent of all persons arrested for this crime were under age eighteen. Of all persons formally processed, 63 percent were referred to juvenile jurisdiction.[9]

Quoting from the FBI report: "One means of measuring the involvement of the young-age group in crime is to identify the number of crimes in which they are offenders. In 1975, 43 percent of the persons processed for Crime Index offenses were young persons referred to juvenile court jurisdiction.[10]

Nationally, persons under fifteen years of age made up nine percent of the total police arrests; under eighteen, 26 percent. Arrests of both males and females under eighteen years of age increased thirteen percent from 1970 to 1975. Arrests of males in the serious crime groups for this period increased 30 percent and female arrests increased by 56 percent.

In 1975 police arrests for all offenses except traffic increased two percent over 1974. During this time, arrests of persons under eighteen years of age increased two percent and arrests of persons over eighteen years of age increased three percent. During the five-year period arrests of young people under eighteen years of age were up thirteen percent.

Using only Crime Index offenses for computing the five-year trend, the arrests of young persons under eighteen years of age increased 27 percent. "Violent crime arrests for persons under eighteen years of age increased 54 percent while the property crime arrests increased 24 percent."[11]

It must be recognized that not all persons arrested are handed over to the courts for prosecution.... For example about one-half of the juvenile arrests are handled by the individual law enforcement agencies without preferring a formal charge or referring them directly to juvenile authorities.... Forty-three percent of all persons processed for Crime Index offenses were young persons referred to juvenile court jurisdiction. Sixty-three percent of those processed for motor vehicle theft were juveniles. Juvenile referrals for burglary were 57 percent, larceny 40 percent, robbery 37 percent, forcible rape 21 percent, aggravated assault 18 percent and murder 9 percent.[12]

The *Crime Report* includes a Table entitled: "Total Arrests of Persons Under 15, Under 18, and Under 25 Years of Age, 1975." Statistics recorded are from 8,051 agencies which work with an estimated population of 179,191,000. The following statistics are reported from Table 37.

The grand total arrests for violent crimes for this age group was 370,453. Violent crimes include offenses of murder, forcible rape, robbery and aggravated assault. Of this grand total 24,166 or 6.5 percent arrests were of persons under fifteen years of age. A total of 85,418 or 23.1 percent of arrests were of persons under eighteen years of age.

Property crimes, which include offenses of burglary, larceny, theft and motor vehicle theft, accounted for 1,528,317 arrests. Of this grand total 299,974 or 19.6 percent arrests were of persons under age fifteen. Persons under age eighteen accounted for 733,775 or 48.0 percent of arrests in this category.

Information contained in the same Table indicates a total of 14,589 arrests for arson. Of this grand total 4,094 or 33.6 percent arrests were of persons under the age of fifteen. Persons under the age of eighteen accounted for 7,727 or 53 percent of arrests for this offense.

Stolen property, buying, receiving, selling, was also an offense with a high percentage of juvenile arrests indicated. Total arrests for 1975 were 100,903. Of this grand total 9,445 young people or 9.4 percent were under age fifteen. Persons under age eighteen accounted for 32,891 or 32.6 percent of the arrests.

Vandalism can almost be thought of as exclusively a young person's violation. A grand total of 175,865 arrests were made in 1975 of young people under twenty-five for this offense. Of this grand total, 66,663 or 37.9 percent of the young people arrested were under the age of fifteen. The under age eighteen group comprised 115,046 or 65.4 percent of the arrests for this violation.

Arrests for narcotic drug law violations for this age group totaled 508,189. Of this total 16,229 or 3.2 percent arrests were of young persons under the age of fifteen. For those young persons under the age of eighteen the report indicates a total number of arrests of 122,857 or 24.2 percent.

There has been some indication that the trend reveals a decrease of narcotics violations and a heavy increase in consumption of alcohol. This report indicates a total of 267,057 arrests of persons under twenty-five for the violation of liquor laws. This does not include drunkenness. Of this grand total 9,429 or 3.5 percent of arrests were of persons under fifteen; 105,813 or 39.6 percent of arrests were of persons under eighteen. Drunkenness accounted for the arrest of 1,176,121 persons under the age of twenty-five. Of this total 4,243 or .4 percent were youths under the age of fifteen; 41,457 or 3.5 percent were of persons under the age of eighteen.

Of all arrests for loitering and curfew violations, a total of 112,117, the arrests were of persons under the age of eighteen, with 26.7 percent of all arrested under the age of fifteen.

During 1975, according to statistical data recorded in this Table, 188,817 arrests were made of runaways. These were of young people under the age of eighteen, with 40.4 percent of all arrests of runaways being of persons under the age of fifteen.

Young people are carrying weapons. As recorded by the FBI, of the 130,933 arrests made during 1975 of young persons under age twenty-five, 5,127 or 3.9 percent were of persons under age fifteen, and 21,365 or 16.3 percent were of persons under age eighteen.

One hundred seventy-seven or .4 percent of the total arrests made for prostitution and commercialized vice in this age group were of persons under the age of fifteen. Persons under age eighteen accounted for a total of 2,362 or 4.7 percent of arrests for this offense.[13]

The *Crime Report* as submitted by the Director of the FBI for the year 1975 does indicate a definite increase in the juvenile delinquency rate. The rate of increase has been most significant over the past five years. The alarming fact is that not all offenses are reported.

Locally, the Pierce County Juvenile Court, Tacoma, Washington, has over five thousand referrals a year. Not all are referred for an alleged delinquent act, but many are. Of the number referred, a large percentage are worked with by the probation officers on an unofficial basis. The numbers referred for official court action are increasing annually.

An alarming observation to be pointed out is that young people are not involved in kid stuff any longer. Many of them are in big time activity. Individual rights and student rights laws have seemingly blinded the senses of right and wrong. It is a dangerous game that is being played and no one seems to have the answer. The offense which seemed to be unthought of five years ago is thought little of today. To be busted or to spend days in detention, to be in a formal court hearing and under the jurisdiction of the probation officer is a status symbol for some young people today. They are looked up to by their peers. They are considered "with it!"

Each segment of society seems to be puzzled by and concerned about the increase of delinquency. School staff is expressing grave concern in this area. An article appearing in the *Parade* section of the *Seattle Post Intelligencer*, dated March 1, 1976 voices concern over school violence.

> Last year American children committed one hundred murders, 12,000 armed robberies, 9,000 rapes and 204,000 aggravated assaults against teachers and fellow students. Children were also responsible for 270,000 school burglaries and vandalized more than $600 million worth of school property.[14]

Who is responsible for these teenage terrorists? *Education U.S.A., Washington Monitor*, dated March 29, 1976 states in an article entitled "Student Rights Need Local, not Federal, Know-How": "Another disturbing trend is that the principal's problems are no longer just traditional discipline concerns but violations of the law .... Smoking in the hall is quite a different problem from a physical assault on a teacher."[15]

The *Tacoma News Tribune*, dated March 21, 1976 carried an article entitled "Spiralling Tyranny of Juvenile Hoods," dateline Washington. The writer, Tom Tiede comments in the article:

America has become a nation where people under the age of 18 commit nearly half of all the known serious crimes, yet juvenile justice and delinquency prevention starve for meaningful concern except by the increasingly numerous victims. Publicize them? Lock them away? It has done no good in the past. And yet neither has the Father Flanigan philosophy that a kid is not responsible for his sins. I confess I haven't the answer for the problem, except to submit that the nation must find itself again, in order for its children to be the same. The alternative is readily apparent — it is where we are heading at the present.[16]

The impact of increased delinquency is felt in many areas which affect the total population in one way or another. Whether directly affected or not, everyone pays a price. Just as it is impossible to present the scope of the problem with total accuracy because of variables, so it is impossible to present the total impact delinquency has on a community or an individual.

The financial impact of juvenile delinquency in any community is great. It is true monetary costs are not as important as other considerations, but this is a factor. The cost of operating juvenile correctional centers, juvenile courts, the loss incurred as a result of offenses committed, the costs for law enforcement, for the arrest and prosecution of these young offenders, runs into millions of dollars each year in any state. Add to that the capital investment of building facilities, maintenance of buildings used in housing these young people, cost of equipment, salaries of staff. The total is unbelievable, and it is increasing annually.

Millions more are spent annually throughout the nation initiating programs, clinics, and various services geared to assist the delinquent or delinquently-oriented child and his family. Social agencies are literally pouring money into preventative programs. The federal government is funding programs which provide employment, recreational facilities, and education for these young people. The philosophy behind all of this seems to be that the child is a victim of society. Society must then pay the price by keeping him occupied, keeping him entertained, keeping him in money, and placing before him the opportunity for an education! Has it worked?

The human impact of juvenile delinquency is the most difficult to assess. What about the impact of delinquency on those who work with these young offenders. It is impossible to work day after day with the problem and not feel the effect. This varies from person to person, depending upon the specific role and degree of involvement and personal philosophy. And what about the impact on the family? The attitudes of the delinquent child spill over into his family. There is discord, and often the family is split.

The most damaging impact of all is that experienced by the young person himself, though he may not be aware of what is happening to him. He cannot possibly live through such experiences without change taking place within himself. His self-image is important. How he sees himself during this involvement and following his involvement is significant for his emotional growth. Very often the first delinquent act is the first step to adult crime. The juvenile record testifies loudly to the fact that juveniles may graduate from delinquency to criminal activity because of the impact of first offenses.

That's the view of the delinquency problem! What can be done? Administrative staff in various states are giving much thought to reforms. Mental health clinics have served at the request of state and local governments in an attempt to meet a need. Diagnostic centers have been established at the state and local level to assist in gaining a better understanding of the problem. Psychological testing, while a valuable aid, has not provided the answer. School districts have attempted to revise and develop new programs in an effort to keep youth in the educational process. Parents and volunteer groups are assisting in the care of children placed in custody of the state. Psychologists and psychiatrists are conducting group therapy sessions and parenting groups, providing counseling, and teaching classes geared to gaining an understanding of how to more effectively work and live with the delinquent child. Groups of children have rallied to the cause and provide entertainment, gifts, and encouragement to children in detention centers.

The reform gaining momentum in Washington State at the moment is the establishing of community-based rehabilitation centers, known as group homes, or in some instances, foster homes. If this system becomes operational, the State Diagnostic Center and the state housing facilities for the young would close. Each county would be responsible for establishing its own diagnostic program. The state contends such an arrangement would be a great saving to the taxpayer. The annual cost of institutional care per person in a state facility in Washington State is approximately $24,500. The cost for a group home for the year is much less. But there are disadvantages. The young person may not receive the treatment in a group home that he needs and could receive in a state facility. The school districts do not have programs which will meet the needs of many of these young people. The community does not appear to be ready to agree to residential housing. The feeling is that the community needs and expects protection from some of these young people.

The county administrators indicate the costs would be more than the local government could bear and that supplemental monies would not be forthcoming indefinitely.

The view of the delinquency problem and human solutions is distressing. But delinquency is not the only juvenile problem. Dependency rates are also increasing annually. The needs of these children have not received the widespread publicity needed to call attention to their plight. Various professional groups have organized in an effort to educate the public as to what is really going on.

The runaway, for example, may now call a number and leave a message for parents. This kind of assistance is offered both in the interests of the child and the parent. Involvement is left to the discretion of the runaway. No pressure is exerted by the one answering the call. Parents spend sleepless nights worrying and wondering where the child may be. Such a message may be of great comfort to the parent.

Incorrigible children are being provided for through group home and foster care placement. Children involved as status offenders present the greatest challenge to workers in the field. It is most difficult to make gains with many of these children. Parents become discouraged because of willful disobedience. The child becomes disenchanted with the home because his parents never seem to understand. In open court family members often verbally express a love for one another, but it is evident they are unable to work together. The court has difficulty keeping such a home intact.

Children's Protective Services report annually increasing rates of cases of abused and neglected children. In Tacoma, Washington the report from the local CPS office indicates 125 to 130 referrals each month, the total number of children involved with the referrals being around 300. Of this group 75 percent will have been referred because of neglect and 25 percent for sexual or physical abuse. Investigations do not always call for prosecution or intervention by the court.

The impact of dependency cannot be ignored. From an economic point of view, it is very costly. Many of these children are placed outside the home. Parents cannot afford to contribute more than a small amount, if any, for this care. The balance is paid with state welfare funds.

Psychological damage to the child cannot be measured. This is the most significant impact to be considered. Many children are so damaged by the time they are brought to the attention of the court that they suffer for as long as they live. As adults they are not able to function adequately because of these experiences in childhood. Long range therapy is required in some cases. Even this is not always successful.

The scars on the body are visible. The scar on the heart cannot be seen except by God.

The problem seems overwhelming. Solutions seem to be stop-gap measures at best, as the rates of juvenile delinquency and dependency increase annually.

Notes, Chapter 11

[1] U.S., Federal Bureau of Investigation, Clarence M. Kelley, Director, *Uniform Crime Reports, Crime in the United States, 1975*, released August 25, 1976, p. 48.

[2] Ibid., p. 48.
[3] Ibid., p. 15.
[4] Ibid., p. 20.
[5] Ibid., pp. 22-24.
[6] Ibid., pp. 24-26.
[7] Ibid., pp. 26-31.
[8] Ibid., pp. 31-34.
[9] Ibid., pp. 34-37.
[10] Ibid., p. 42.
[11] Ibid., p. 41.
[12] Ibid., p. 42.
[13] Ibid., p. 190.
[14] *Seattle Post Intelligencer*, 1 March 1976.

[15] "Student Rights Need Local, not Federal, Know-How," *Education U.S.A., Washington Monitor*, 29 March 1976, p. 185.

[16] Tom Tiede, "Spiralling Tyranny of Juvenile Hoods," *The Tacoma News Tribune*, 21 March 1976.

Chapter 12:

Causes and Responsibilities

Barbara has just been charged and adjudged a sexual delinquent. A strikingly beautiful girl even in her emaciated condition, Barbara ran from home five months ago, living with whoever offered her shelter. She left home, she explained, because she could not tolerate her mother's "shacking up" with "every guy that comes along." She soon learned that food and clothes are not free, neither is a bed free — it is often shared. She also needed drugs. So she did the thing that had worked for her mother — she exchanged her body for food, clothing, a shared bed, and drugs. This kind of life took its toll. She had a venereal disease; she had aborted once. She was tired. She had no fight left. "Do whatever you have to — just let me sleep! I don't care what happens. I won't go home. Just send me wherever you want to!"

What caused Barbara to reach this point in her life? Who is responsible for her?

At seventeen Jim was before the court on a waiver of jurisdiction. Since age eleven he had been involved in auto theft, burglary, drinking, driving without a license, drug use, vandalism. Finally, he took a gun from a home he burglarized and held up a store. When the owner resisted, Jim shot him. The man lived, but may suffer permanent damage. The juvenile system has nothing more to offer. Jurisdiction was declined. Jim was tried as an adult, convicted, and sent to the adult correctional center.

What caused Jim to reach this point in his life? Who shares the responsibility?

Bobby and Cindy are seated before the judge. Their little bodies carry the marks of severe beatings. School personnel called authorities when they arrived at school in that condition, and they were entered at the Hall. The parents were furious. Their reason for discipline: "Kids have got to be made to mind. My dad gave me a good whipping when I needed it. It didn't hurt me." Bobby and Cindy cry. They love their parents and want to go home. They tell of receiving beatings almost every day. The judge orders placement outside the home, and counseling for parents and children.

What caused these children to be in this situation? Who is responsible in working this through?

Case after case, each tearing at the heart in its own particular way. But each must be dealt with. The questions asked must be answered.

What are the causes for delinquency? Many reasons have been suggested through the years — sociological, psychological, physiological. The behavioral science field has proposed the premise that the child's behavior is conditioned by the influences of the society within which he lives. Such a deterministic theory would seem to preclude personal opportunities for learning and growth, for decision-making and self-responsibility. Environmental factors do have impact in shaping a life. A child is the product of various stimuli. But he is not a puppet pulled in any direction at the will of another. At one point in his life he begins to make decisions, and he must be held accountable for these decisions. Such a theory extends also to parents who are child abusers. The parent is seen as a victim of a deprived childhood, an abused person himself. The literature developed by organizations working with abusers cautions workers to deal gently with the person, to avoid direct questions, irritation, and direct discussion of the problem. Does the theory that the parent or a delinquent is a victim of circumstances mean that he should not be held responsible, that he has no control over his behavior?

Some professionals attempt to trace the causes of delinquency using the psychodynamics within the family. The interaction of the children with parents, or child with parent, parent with child, or children, is pointed out as the basis of the problem. While family interaction cannot be ignored when working with a child, neither can it be used as the only basis to determine the cause of delinquent behavior. Broken family structure is also given as the cause of delinquency. Family structure is important. But many children who live in one-parent homes are not delinquent. Working mothers has also been proposed as a reason for a child being delinquent. Divorce and remarriage has often been quoted as "tearing the child apart, causing him to do the things he does." These reasons are significant, but are they the total reason?

Other sociological causes given are neighborhood conditions and economic level. "We have to move out of that neighborhood. That's why he is in trouble!" Many sociologists feel delinquency is concentrated in certain living areas. "We aren't able to give her the things she wants — like other kids have — so she takes them." Low economic level may be an explanation for delinquency, but is it an excuse? What about the hundreds of other youngsters living under similar circumstances who never break the law?

The schools are also blamed. Parents blame school staff for "allowing" their child to skip school, leave the grounds and commit a burglary, steal a car, or what have you. "Schools don't teach them respect for the law and for other people's property." "Not enough discipline in the schools." No one can deny that the school does have an influence on a child. But what is the role of the school and how far can the school go in carrying out this role?

Urbanization and social change are also blamed. "Times have changed" we hear as the reason for an upsurge in delinquency. The pressures of social change are too great for the child to bear.

"Nothing to do" is worn out as a reason given by young people in trouble. "We got bored, so we just went out ...." Yes, went out and vandalized, burglarized, used drugs, stole cars, or committed acts of sexual delinquency. Is it the responsibility of the society to be sure that each child is entertained every waking hour? What happened to household chores and good reading or homework?

Besides sociological reasons given for the increase in juvenile delinquency, psychological disorders are cited. "He has emotional problems." "He needs psychiatric care." "He doesn't feel good about himself." "He does not feel he is loved." "He is loved too much, spoiled." "He needs to get his head on straight." Disobedience is often interpreted as "an emotional problem." Breaking the law is often interpreted as a reaction to an emotional hang-up. Rarely do court personnel hear a parent say, "He stole the car because he is a thief." We do hear judges say, "Your emotions are showing because you got caught, not because you did not know what you were doing!" Personality disorders, when diagnosed as such by professionals, such as psychologists and psychiatrists, are certainly a determinant of types of behavior. But this is easily recognizable by the act committed. Sociopathic disorders will cause a great deal of hostility and aggressive behavior to emerge. The sociopath usually seeks immediate gratification of his need. But this differs distinctly from the child who just wants something and takes it. Personality disorders are complex and must be explained and worked with by trained specialists in the field. Through psychological tests these problems are pin-pointed and reported to the court.

Hereditary and physiological factors are often discussed as a possible cause for delinquency. To what extent heredity influences behavior is not known. To say that it is the major contributing factor to behavior would preclude other influences.

Does any one of these theories — sociological, psychological, or physiological — give an answer to the question: What is the cause for the increased rates in juvenile delinquency and dependency? Does any one of these theories answer the question of why a child suffers abuse or neglect at the hands of a parent? Does any one of these theories answer the question as to why there is an increase in incorrigibility and runaway rates?

Who is responsible for working to correct the situation?

The home certainly plays a major role. Behavior is learned. The first influences in the child's life come from family interaction. The child must experience love, security, a sense of self worth and a feeling of belonging in his home. But with this he must be disciplined to learn self-discipline. A disciplined child knows right from wrong. He must learn to make a contribution to the family through his own efforts. He must learn to respect the rights of others. He must learn to be accountable, and to be responsible for the decisions he makes. He has the right to expect care and protection from his parents, and he has the responsibility to be a productive member of that family. The home needs to provide spiritual guidance for the child. God mandated certain responsibilities to parents and established guidelines for carrying out these responsibilities.

The church cannot avoid responsibility. Very few churches have established programs to meet the needs of this group of children. Many of these children would respond to efforts made by individuals or groups within the church. Juvenile court staff is usually willing to accept assistance from any group or individual. So there are opportunities for interaction. The church appears to be asleep. It must take a stand against this permissive behavior.

The school is involved. Many delinquent acts occur within the school during school hours. Discipline is not the same in schools as it used to be. The reasons given are varied. Some staff say that student rights laws prohibit control of students. Another reason given is that parents are not supportive. Or, various community groups "will be on our back." Another is that there are no programs in the public school which meet the needs of many of these children. Children tend to do what is expected of them. Are we actually selling them short? If a child needs to be disciplined, the school authority should mete out discipline without such a hassle from the home or the community. Student rights laws do not prohibit accountability and responsibility on the part of the student. In fact, if procedure is followed, they insure this. One thing I am sure of and that is that those of us in education share in this responsibility. We cannot do it all, but we certainly should acknowledge we are a part of it.

It is also a community problem. Law enforcement, social agencies, the judiciary — no one is exempt. Despite the good intentions, many of the programs and plans devised by some social agencies have had a damaging effect. The buck is passed from state departments responsible for rehabilitative care to the local community, and back again. Young people are being returned to the community before they are ready to take their place in society. Consequently, they come before the court very soon again because of delinquent behavior. It may be a status symbol to "get busted"; it may be smart to "beat the rap"; and it may be "cool" to "be in", but the blue denim generation of today are really the losers. Adults are paying a price also. But if we see it, we are not willing to acknowledge it to the point of taking definite positive action. Doesn't it make sense to say that adults should really be setting the standards and dealing positively with violations rather than turning our backs or at best using superficial remedies? Could the answer be that we are not individually equipped to deal with the problem? We don't have what it takes to assume this responsibility!

For an interesting answer to the above questions, ask any young person. The answer may surprise some. It may shock others. Try it!

Chapter 13:

The Christian Answer; The Christian's Responsibility

It had been a long, emotion-packed day in court. The judge had heard twenty-one cases. The expression on his face revealed his physical weariness. The decisions he had made would carry tremendous impact on many lives.

Sixteen year old John had been before the court that day, brought to the attention of the court by his mother. John had barricaded himself in his room each night, and sometimes for the full day. She could hear a hammer pounding, then all would be quiet. She could not enter. He had a lock on the door. She called for assistance. When the police entered the room, they found John had built a casket in his closet. The entry to the box was a small door at one end which John crawled through. This opening could be locked from the inside. The closet door also had a lock on the inside. John would lock himself in the closet, crawl in the casket, and spend many hours shut out from the world. He would not eat. He refused to communicate with the family. John had little to say to the judge. There was very little the judge could say to him. "We are going to try to help you, John. We are going to send you where doctors and others can work with you, where you can be helped to get back on your feet. You have a lot to offer. We need young men with your ability. You will try your best, won't you?"

Charles is eight. He kills animals — cats, dogs, chickens, whatever he can find. He kills them by hanging, skinning, burning, or cutting off parts of the body, one by one, and at different times. A loner, he wanders around the neighborhood at all hours. He enters homes. He steals food for the most part; at times he steal knives and matches. He has been referred to the mental health clinic, private psychiatrists, and for counseling sessions. He has received every service the school district has to offer. He is deteriorating.

Mandi is seven, Susie six, Debbie three, Ted five, and Frank eighteen months of age. Children's Protective Services staff has filed a petition alleging neglect and unfit home. The investigation reveals the children are left alone for days at a time. There is no food in the house. They beg from neighbors. The house is filthy. Broken plumbing. Animal feces on the floors throughout. Urine-soaked mattresses full of holes. No lights. Service had been discontinued months before. Clothing is scant, dirty, and in need of repair. The parents drink heavily, take frequent trips out of town to visit friends, and spend a great deal of time at the tavern and bingo parlors.

Sam is seventeen. He has been using drugs for years. On a bad trip, he ran from his home nude, and broke through the glass sliding doors of a nearby residence. He was cut over a major portion of his body. He ran to the bathroom and barricaded himself, and turned the water on hot. Screaming from the pain of the cuts and hot water, he was finally subdued by police and taken to the hospital.

An escapee from an institutional setting where he had been committed for armed robbery, Carl kidnapped a woman and her two children. He knocked on the door early one morning. When the lady opened it, he asked to use the phone. Once inside the house, he pulled a gun. He forced the lady and the children to leave with him. A wild ride ensued. The woman and children were threatened with death if they attempted to escape. Low on gas, he stopped at a station. An alert attendant called police, sensing something was wrong. Carl challenged the police with the gun, but was overpowered and surrendered. "You are going to come to the end of the line one day, and I am afraid it won't be pleasant. I see no future for you. You will destroy yourself." The judge's prediction came true. Carl was killed one night following his release from the penitentiary. He was shot attempting to break into a home.

"What got into you?" the judge asks. "I don't get it. I just don't get it. Well, I don't have a crystal ball and I don't have all the answers. But there must be an answer!"

Yes, there is an answer. But not all will accept it. Many will continue breaking the law as juveniles. Many parents will continue to weep bitterly. Opportunity after opportunity will be provided for change. Promises will be made. But there will be no change.

The reason is simple. The change must come from within. Social agencies with all their programs and assistance are not the answer. Federal and state laws establishing guidelines for juvenile court structure will not be enough. The sociologists, psychologists, psychiatrists, the judiciary, and the educators have been sincere in their efforts to cope with the problem, but there has been no gain.

During these past years, working very closely with the juvenile court, with troubled children, grief-stricken parents, and with community agencies, I have learned much. I have a great deal more to learn, but there is one strong conviction I have. Man's philosophies which leave God out are doomed for failure. The evidence is here as we look at the spiralling rate of juvenile delinquency and dependency. As we view the programs proposed to curb these problems, as we review the laws and guidelines, we have to admit we are not seeing the job done.

I believe we are reaping the harvest of a total and complete rejection of God over the past fifty years. It has caught up with us. I am convinced there is no solution to the problem apart from the Lord Jesus Christ. This problem, which is world wide, can be resolved on an individual basis, and only on an individual basis. When the individual recognizes his need of a Savior and receives the Lord Jesus Christ, he receives the only remedy for sin. He receives the only One who is able to change him. Christ specializes in new creations: "If any man be in Christ, he is a new creature" (II Corinthians 5:17). New priorities are set, a different pattern of life is organized, and real purpose is found which allows no room for defrauding any one in any way, either by a violation of the law, by personal harm to another, or by harm to one's self.

Often I hear a young person plead for one more chance — just one more chance to make good. But judicial acquittal will never free a young person, nor will it ever free anyone. Freedom is a cherished and sought after possession. True freedom can only be found in Christ. "And you shall know the truth and the truth shall make you free" (John 8:32). Divine liberation alone brings true freedom.

The law has standards which must be met. So does God. The law has a penalty for not meeting the standard. So does God. As I have watched a juvenile court judge attempting to work out a legal solution which would allow the child and his family another opportunity, I recall how God worked in my own behalf when He judged my sin at the cross. He sent His Son to pay my penalty. "For he hath made him to be sin for us, who knew no sin; that we might be made the righteousness of God in him" (II Corinthians 5:21). Because of Christ's shed blood, I do not carry the guilt of sin any longer. By accepting in simple faith what Christ did for me at the cross, I am free.

Divine liberation! The juvenile court judge, powerful though he may be, does not have this power!

As I continue to watch the judge, I am also reminded of another judgment recorded in God's Word. As the young person is told by the judge: "You must be accountable for your actions," God tells me in His Word: "For we must appear before the judgment seat of Christ; that every one may receive the things done in his body, according to that he has done, whether it be good or bad" (II Corinthians 5:10). Accountability has almost become a word of the past — something we can look up in the dictionary if we know the spelling. "My rights" has become the substitute. But the judgment of the juvenile court judge is made on that basis — not on intentions, not on what influences were at play, but on personal involvement. God works that way also. We are going to account for our actions before God one day and some of our excuses are going to be rather feeble. "That's not my belief." "I had to go to church when I was young, I had enough of it then." "Who says a loving God would do that?" "I just don't see it that way — I just think if you do the best you can do, it doesn't matter what you believe, just so you believe it."

"You have had your chance, you refused to obey, and now I must deal with you!" How often I have heard the judge remind the young offender in words similar to these. The judgment of the court is now a necessity. Provision was made for an opportunity to do something about the way of life, to change, to establish a new value system which would preclude the breaking of the law, but it has not been taken advantage of. When I witness such an event in court, I am reminded of another judgment in the Word of God. I tremble as I read the words recorded in Revelation 20:11–15:

> And I saw a great white throne, and him that sat on it, from whose face the earth and the heaven fled away; and there was found no place for them. And I saw the dead, small and great, stand before God; and the books were opened; and another book was opened, which is the book of life: and the dead were judged out of those things which were written in the books, according to their works. And the sea gave up the dead which were in it: and death and hell delivered up the dead that were in them: and they were judged every man according to their works. And death and hell were cast into the lake of fire. This is the second death. And whosoever was not found written in the book of life was cast into the lake of fire.

The Great White Throne Judgment — where all who have rejected Christ will face the Great Judge, God Himself! There will be no second chance! The judgment of the juvenile court is awesome. But there are no words to express this judgment. God has said it: eternal separation from Him.

God has provided an opportunity. But even if Christ Himself should walk among us, as He did when He was here on earth, there would be the scoffers and those who would refuse to believe even today. Just as the juvenile court judge, when warning after warning has been ignored and the violation of the law continued, can give no more chances, so God has warned us many times. He has allowed every opportunity for each individual to make things right with Him. To ignore Him will only lead to judgment.

As I observe the interaction of the judge and the young offender, I sometimes want to say to the child, "Why won't you learn? You are really asking for it, and now you are going to get it." But then I am reminded of how we so glibly ignore the power of a Higher Court and an Almighty Judge.

PLEASE RISE!

The juvenile court judge has entered the court room. Respect his position! Respect his authority! He is in control. This young life is in his hands. By the authority vested in him by the state, he is charged with the responsibility of making a disposition within the framework of the legal statutes of the state. His law demands. But he cannot change a life! Every young person who enters the juvenile court, every parent of every child who is before the court, along with every living soul, shall one day face the only Life-Changer, either as Lord and Savior, or as Judge. My responsibility is to share this with others. My responsibility extends to the juvenile offender, to his parents, and beyond to my colleagues, to my friends, and now to you, my reader . . . .

PLEASE RISE!

It may be that you are concerned about how life has been going for you. Perhaps you have been depending on programs. It may be you have never heard of the Person who has the answer to your problem. If that is true, and you have never received Jesus Christ as your Savior, you may do so just now, in simple faith, just taking Him at His word: "For God so loved the world that he gave his only begotten Son, that whosoever believeth in him should not perish, but have everlasting life. For God sent not his Son into the world to condemn the world; but that the world through him might be saved." These are God's words, as recorded in John's Gospel, chapter 3. He goes on to say, "He that believeth on him is not condemned: but he that believeth not is condemned already, because he has not believed in the name of the only begotten Son of God" (John 3:16–18). The most heinous crime ever committed, the crucifixion of Jesus Christ, God's Son, was turned into the greatest blessing by God the Father. He used this crime to display His marvelous grace and love and to bring us so full salvation. The law demands; God's grace beseeches! He will not force anyone. We may reject now, but one day "at the name of Jesus every knee should bow ... and every tongue confess that Jesus Christ is Lord, to the glory of God" (Philippians 2:10–11).

PLEASE RISE!

Perhaps you, as a Christian, have been concerned about your own responsibility. It may be that you are a pastor of a church that should have a concern for this segment of our population and reach out in a positive way in working with them. It may be that as a member of a church you have been concerned about the role you should take in working with delinquent and dependent youth in your area. As you have read the case studies and felt the need, perhaps the Lord has spoken to your heart and is directing you to become involved. Perhaps you are not sure where to begin, or how you might serve. Let me make some suggestions.

For the pastor. There are opportunities within the missionary outreach of the church for reaching these young people. Establish within the missionary program a plan of ministry which will allow regular contacts with the youth center in your city or county. By prayerful selection, appoint a director or chairman of this group. Then take your concerns to the administrators in charge of the youth facility and offer your services. It has been my experience that church groups have been welcomed. This contact provides a resource for the staff of the juvenile court. Frequently, in my experience, I have known of young people and parents who have requested a visit from a minister, or a member of the church. They have no church home. You could be that pastor or representative for the Lord to serve in this way. Suggest your availability to serve as chaplain of the facility. Set aside an evening during the week or a Sunday afternoon for ministering to the youth residing in the youth center. Young people from the church may be used to sing and to give brief testimonies during the service. Youth responds to youth.

For church groups and individuals. Cookies are always a welcome treat at the youth centers. The ladies of the church may share in this by providing, not only for the service, but on a regular basis. Youth groups and other organized groups within the church could take on a project to meet a specific need, such as dental equipment, supplies for the medical center, clothing for the children, supplies for the school program operating within the facility, a sum of money for the children's fund. Gifts for the children at Christmas time and birthdays are always needed.

Volunteer workers are always needed in such facilities. Children frequently need to be transported to the doctor or dentist, or they need to be taken out to purchase needed items of clothing. Children need hair cuts, shampoos, and sets. Secretarial help is needed — phone answering, intake desk services, filing, gathering of statistical data. Supervision of play times requires adult volunteers. Games such as ping-pong and sit-down games — anything that serves to occupy time and provide interaction will also provide opportunity for witness. Volunteer services are usually coordinated by a designated staff member who can be contacted by phone.

For the church family. As a church family you may wish to consider one of the great needs — group homes and foster homes. Church-sponsored group homes would provide opportunity to meet the spiritual needs of some of these children in addition to the material needs. State and federal monies may be available to support such a project. Guidelines for writing proposals in applying for such funds are available to interested groups. In addition to group homes, Christian homes are needed for foster care — interim or long term. This need could be met through organized effort within the church body, or on an individual basis. Certification for such care within a home is usually done through the welfare department in each area. Guidelines for applying are available upon request.

Church families, or groups, may wish to "adopt" a child living in the juvenile hall as a dependent. Letters, books, articles of clothing, and visits are ways of making contributions. The association would not have to be terminated when the child is placed, but could continue, especially if the child is placed within the community. The policy of the court with which I am associated is that a child is not allowed to make periodic visits in a home unless that home is a possible foster placement. This is understandable. These children are so anxious to be loved and accepted, that they become attached to anyone who reaches out to them. Such an experience could be too traumatic. But the building of a relationship outside of the home setting is acceptable.

As you become aware of possibilities for personal involvement, you will be able to add to the list. If your situation prohibits active involvement, you can pray. Your prayers of concern will allow the Lord to touch the hearts of those who can serve and will open doors of opportunity for these children to hear the gospel. Christ is the answer, but how can they believe when they have not heard? Pray for guidance and direction in your own life as you think of the needs of our delinquent and dependent youth. There is a place of service available for you.

For parents. As a parent, perhaps you are troubled by what you have read. You may be concerned about relating to your own child in such a way that will avoid his becoming involved with the court.

Be a parent. If you are a Christian the Word of God has specifically defined the role of each family member. As a father, you are charged with the responsibility to be the head, or the leader in your home. As a mother, you are to assist in this effort. So often differences in childrearing practices are the basis for many problems. Together establish guidelines for your home, guidelines that are fair and known by all members of the family. Reasonable consequences should be established for the violation of reasonable expectations. Be consistent. This lays the groundwork for security needed by all children. Listen to your child. You may be surprised what you hear. Observe your child. Get to know him. Be aware of his interests. Know his friends. Know his whereabouts. Respect him as an individual. Being in control does not mean a parent is to be unreasonably controlling. Allow for individual growth under the guidance of understanding and discriminating love. Under the direction of the Holy Spirit be an example to your child. Pray for him; show him by your actions your faith in the Lord. Lead him in such a way that he too will have a close, personal walk with the Lord. As he observes your sense of responsibility, he learns responsibility; as he experiences fair, reasonable discipline, he learns self-discipline; he learns respect for others and the law as he observes your attitudes. Through a demonstration of your love, based on God's principles, he learns the importance of love, of belonging, of feeling secure, and of experiencing success which provides a basis for self-worth. Entrust your child to the Lord, and make sure you are living as the Lord directs.

For the young person. Are you fighting a battle within yourself about your responsibilities within the home and community? There is a price to pay for disobedience. There is great gain in establishing a right relationship within the family structure, but more importantly to the Lord. Take a few moments' time, really level with yourself. Are you where you should be? How do you feel about yourself? What kind of person are you? Really, no faking it? If you feel the need, get yourself straightened out. The Lord can do it for you, but you must be willing. You are needed in a real way in helping young people who are court connected. Won't you share in this responsibility?

The answer will never be found in a program. It is found in a Person! The answer will never be found collectively. It will of necessity need to be found individually!

Appendices

Appendix 1

Historical Background of the Juvenile Justice System

Early beginnings of the juvenile justice system were established as a part of the judiciary in England in the late 18th century. The Court of Chancery was considered an "equity court" to assist the king in his role as *parens patrae*, or the parent of the country. No distinction was made between adult and juvenile justice but the concept of individual justice was operative and the judge became the parent, or the substitute for the child's inadequate family.

Steps leading to the establishment of the Juvenile Justice System in America:

1825—House of Refuge in New York State. Warehouses were used for holding abandoned children. These were orphanages in effect; children were "rescued" by well-to-do families and used as servants. A concern had begun to grow for the welfare not only of children without a home, but for those who had broken the law. Of major concern was the lack of separation from adult criminals in holding facilities.

1869—Massachusetts established a Board of Charity. An appointed member of this Board was to represent any child under the age of sixteen appearing in criminal court.

1870—Massachusetts made a clear cut legal distinction between juvenile and adult offenders.

1870—New York established a law which would not permit the juvenile offender to be housed with the adult offender.

1899—On April 21, 1899 the Illinois Legislature, Cook County, passed the first Juvenile Court Act. This is believed to be the beginning, or the basis, of what is known throughout the United States as the Juvenile Court Code.

Purposes of the Act passed by the Illinois legislature were to regulate the control of delinquent and dependent children and to control the treatment of these children.

Results were:
- specific court proceedings established;
- court room established for specific purpose of hearing juvenile cases;
- circuit judge appointed to preside;
- summary proceeding established;

- children no longer housed with adult criminals;
- juvenile probation officers appointed for the first time with responsibility to investigate the case, provide information to the court, represent the child in court, and supervise probation.

Changes in Juvenile Codes which have established base of operation for juvenile courts across the nation:

1901—Status offender classified; i.e., incorrigible, runaway, truant, etc. Fitness of institutions dealt with in establishing Board of Inspection.

1905—Funds from county treasuries, rather than state funds, to be used for hiring of probation officers.

1907—Law enacted to provide for the return of committed youth to his home under specific conditions.

Appendix 2

Structure of the Juvenile Court: Example

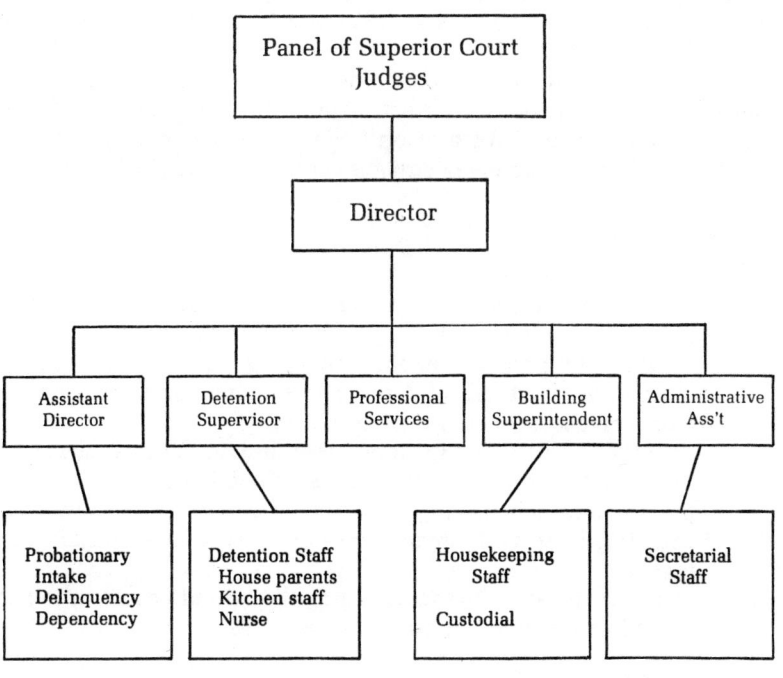

Juvenile Court Law

State of Washington, Chapter 302, RCW 1961, Section I. RCW 13.04. (010–240) This chapter shall be known as the "Juvenile Court Law" and shall apply to all minor children under the age of eighteen years who are delinquent or dependent and to any person or persons who contribute to the delinquency and dependency of such children.

Each state has its own Juvenile Code. In order to provide an example and to create interest for further research, and because of the familiarity with the State of Washington Code the following duties and responsibilities is an example of structure and procedures in this state.

Juvenile Court:

Charged with the responsibility to
- provide for the care, the protection and the moral, mental and physical growth of all children who come within its jurisdiction;
- provide for all delinquent children a program whereby they may receive treatment, rehabilitation and training rather than having them charged with a criminal act;
- only take a child from its home when it is in the best interest of the child or necessary in the interest of public safety;
- provide for a fair hearing for the child where his constitutional and other legal rights are protected in a very simple judicial hearing;
- insure cooperative measures among the juvenile courts in other states by providing interstate compact laws.

Exclusive jurisdiction is granted to the juvenile court in the following proceedings:
- hearings in which the child is alleged to be a delinquent, incorrigible, or dependent as defined by law;
- hearings to terminate parental rights except in instances when this is a part of adoption proceedings;
- hearings to obtain judicial consent for marriage of juveniles;
- hearings to appoint a guardian or determine custody of a child;
- hearings under interstate compact of juveniles;
- hearings on waiver of jurisdiction.

The Juvenile Court Codes of States provide for certain responsibilities and duties to be imposed upon staff. Examples of such in the State of Washington are as follows:

Probation Officers:

Duties:

- to make investigations, reports and recommendations to the juvenile court judge;
- to receive and review complaints of delinquency and dependency;
- to supervise children on probation;
- to make referrals to community agencies when needed;
- to take into custody any child under his supervision if there is reasonable cause to believe that his actions, or that the actions of someone else, is endangering his life, his health or his safety.

Taking the Child into Detention:

A child may be taken in to detention, or custody, if a law enforcement officer has reason to believe that the child is suffering from an illness or injury or is in immediate danger from his surroundings; that he is on the run from his parents, guardian, or custodian, or that he has committed a delinquent act.

Detention of the Child:

A child shall not be held in custody prior to a hearing unless this is necessary for his protection, for the protection of someone else, or the property of someone, or if there is a possibility he might be removed from the jurisdiction of the court.

Release of the Child:

The probation officer, or the person who takes the child into custody, may release the child to his parents, guardian or other custodian prior to a hearing provided there is assurance the child will be delivered to the court upon request; if it is in the best interest of the child he may be held in a detention facility, a medical facility or a shelter care facility pending the hearing. In this case the parent, guardian or custodian shall be provided with a reason as to why the child is held; if the child is released to parent, guardian or custodian and not delivered to the court upon request a warrant may be issued directing that the child be taken into custody and brought before the court.

The court may then make the appropriate placement necessary for the care, protection and control of the child.

Court Placement Locations:

A child taken into custody and alleged to be delinquent may be placed in:

- a home approved by the court — his parents, foster or group care (approved and licensed by the appropriate agency), or relative placement;
- a state detention facility under the supervision of the state.

The unruly, or dependent child may be placed in:
- a licensed foster or group home;
- parents' home under supervision of designated agency;
- any other place the court finds to be suitable.

Detention Procedure:

No child shall be held in detention or shelter longer than 72 hours excluding Sundays and holidays, unless a petition has been filed. No child shall be held more than 72 hours after the filing of a petition unless a court order has been entered for such continued detention or shelter. No child shall be held for longer than 30 days unless detention is authorized by a court order which sets forth the findings upon which the continued detention is based.

Hearing Procedure:

Notice and summons shall be served at least three days prior to hearing upon the child and all persons designated by statute;

The notice shall include time, place, date of hearing and make specific reference to the petition on file (a copy of which is delivered);

The notice shall make a statement as to the purpose of the hearing, the right to remain silent, and the right to representation by counsel, retained or provided.

Petition:

Shall only be filed when the probation officer or person authorized by the court to do so, determines that this is in the best interest of the child. A petition may be filed by any person who has knowledge of the facts or who believes certain facts to be true.

Contents of the Petition:
- states the facts which allegedly brought the child before the court;
- gives name, age, and residence of child;
- gives name, address and residence of parent, guardian or custodian if known and if not, the name of a relative that is known.

Conduct of Hearing:
- Informal, without jury, separate from other proceedings;

- Facts presented by probation officer unless prosecutor does so in support of the petition;
- proceedings shall be recorded by approved means of the court;
- only those directly involved in the hearing shall be present;
- child may be excluded at discretion of the court;
- child has right to counsel, retained or appointed;
- child has right to produce evidence and be heard in his own defense if charged with a delinquent act.

Classification of Hearings:

Detention Hearing:

The child and parents or guardian have the right to be informed that they may request a detention hearing. The court shall hold one if requested. The child, parent or custodian shall be given notice of the time, place and purpose of the hearing. If the written notice of rights and copy of the petition have not already been given to the child, parent or custodian the judge shall do so at the detention hearing. At any detention hearing the child, parent, guardian, or custodian shall have the right to present evidence and be heard on the issue of temporary detention.

If the right to such a hearing is waived the order for the continued temporary detention or shelter shall be signed without a hearing.

Fact-Finding Hearing:

Adjudication hearings where facts are heard to determine finding of delinquency or dependency. If facts are not found to be true beyond a reasonable doubt, either by admission, or presentation of evidence, the petition may be dismissed and the child released. If facts are found to be true, the child is found to be delinquent or dependent as the case may be.

Dispositional Hearing:

Usually follows the fact-finding hearing. The judge may:
- order probation;
- order probation on a suspended commitment;
- commit to the Department of Institutions;
- continue the dispositional hearing for a period of time;
- return the child to his home;
- place him in foster or group care, or send him to live with relatives.

Appeal:
- may be made by the aggrieved part;

- is made to the Supreme Court;
- filing of written notice within thirty days after entry of the order;
- court of general jurisdiction will use files, records, manuscripts from the juvenile court;
- appeal does not stay an order.

Appendix 3

Process Used in the Correction of Juveniles

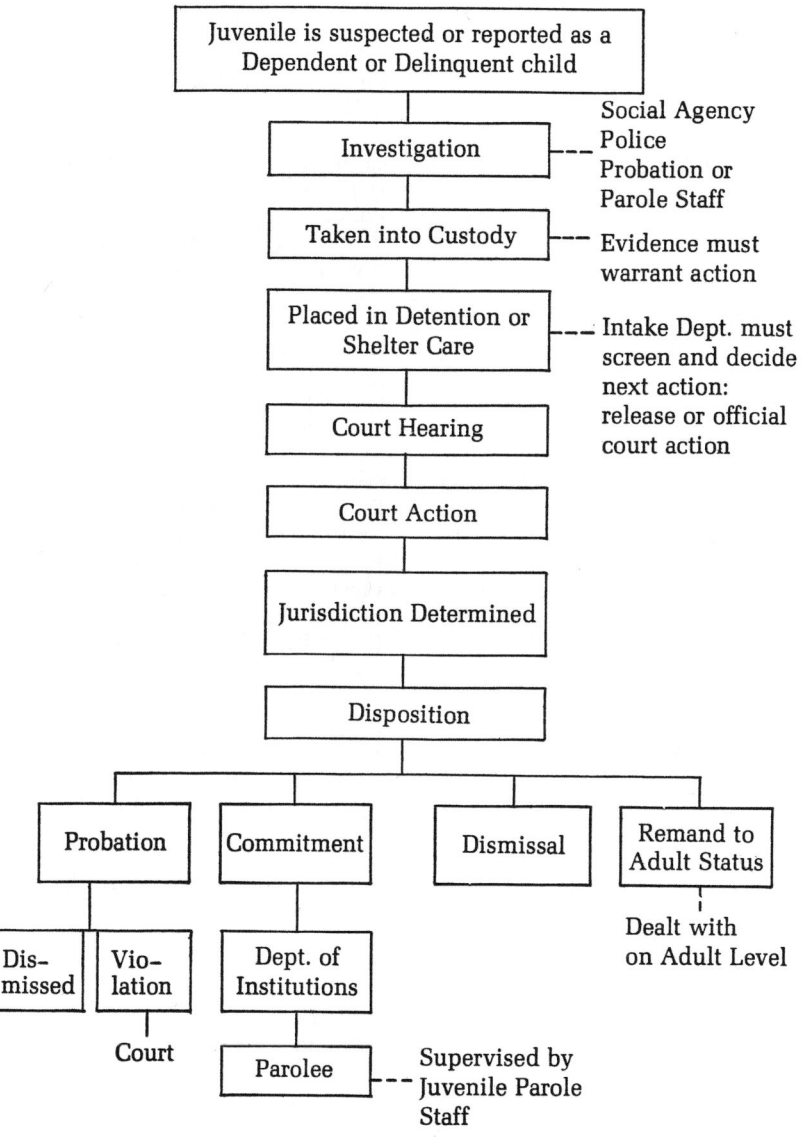

Steps	Those Involved in Transaction (or Participants)
Juvenile is suspected, or is reported as dependent or delinquent child	Parents Individuals in the community Social agencies, such as Welfare, Children's Protective Services, Mental Health Clinics, etc. Public school staff Self-referral
Investigation	Children's Protective Services Dept. of Social & Health Services Police Juvenile Court Probation Officer Juvenile Parole Services staff
Taken into Custody	Police Juvenile Court Probationary staff Juvenile Parole staff Other designated or authorized law enforcement officers
Placed in detention or in shelter care (Intake Officer must make determination for next action—release, or court hearing)	Police Dept. of Social & Health Services Children's Protective Services Juvenile Court Probationary staff Juvenile Parole staff Self-referral Other authorized law enforcement officers
Court Hearing —Detention —Fact Finding —Dispositional	Juvenile Court Probationary staff Juvenile Court Judge Assigned or retained counsel Juvenile (may or may not be present) Witnesses, in some instances Parents, guardians, or custodians, relatives
Court Action —Review of petition	Probation Officer Juvenile Court Judge Prosecuting Attorney Assigned or retained counsel Juvenile Parent, guardian, or custodian

Determines Jurisdiction —Remand to adult status —Retain jurisdiction in Juvenile Court	Probation Officer Prosecutor Judge Assigned or retained counsel Juvenile Parent, guardian or custodian
Disposition (jurisdiction retained by Juvenile Court) —Probation under certain conditions or under a suspended commitment —Commitment to the Department of Institutions —Dismissal of petition —Remand to adult status, to be tried or dealt with on adult level —Violation of probation conditions; return to court for further action —Parolee—returned to community following commitment to Institutions, supervised by Juvenile Parole Staff	Juvenile Court Judge Probation Officer Assigned or retained counsel

Significant Distinctions Between Juvenile and Adult Justice Systems

Juvenile Justice System	Adult Criminal Justice System
Investigation usually by one division within Police Dept. May be done by agency, court or parole staff	Conducted by various divisions within the Police Dept. according to crime committed
Fingerprinting by court order only	Fingerprinting routine
Bail not allowed; detention hearing may be requested	Bail allowed in majority of cases
Decision for court hearing made by probation staff	Prosecutor's office determines prosecutive merit
Civil Court	Criminal Court
Juvenile has a hearing; may have appointed or retained counsel	Adult has a trial; may have appointed or retained counsel
Hearings are closed	Trials are open to the public
No jury hearings; judge makes disposition	Jury trial permissable and procedural in some cases
Adjudicated of delinquency	Convicted of a crime
Loss of freedom	Loss of civil rights and freedom
Less restrictive facilities	Usually restrictive facilities, depending on institutional setting
Emphasis on rehabilitation	Emphasis on rehabilitation and punishment
Duration of stay in institution determined on individual basis	Minimum/maximum term set by statute
Supervision following release	Supervision following release
Records are protected	Records are open

Appendix 4

Laws Significantly Changing the Juvenile Correctional Process

I. *Kent v. United States*, 383 U.S. 541, 16. L. Ed. 2D 84 (1966) Waiver Hearing and due process

Basic safeguards required by due process during the waiver proceedings are:
- the juvenile is entitled to a hearing on the question of waiver;
- the juvenile is entitled to representation by counsel;
- the social record of the juvenile may be reviewed by the attorney prior to the hearing;
- if jurisdiction is waived, the juvenile is entitled to a statement of reasons which support the order of the court.

Commonly used and accepted criteria controlling the transfer decision are as follows:
- whether the juvenile is amenable or suitable for rehabilitation under the juvenile code;
- the welfare of the community; whether the protection of the community would require waiver;
- the nature or seriousness of the offense; prosecutive merit of the case;
- the age, sophistication and maturation of the juvenile, and prior record of the child.

II. *Gault v. United States*, 18. L. Ed. 2D 527 — The requisite fairness and due process placed squarely on the Fourteenth Amendment and used the Bill of Rights as a point of reference in determining the requirements for due process.

Conditions which must be met to insure minimal due process safeguards for all juveniles going through the judicial process in the juvenile court are:
- notice of charges: requires written notice of specific allegations to be heard by the court and to include date, time, and place of such hearing;
- the right to counsel: at any hearing which may result in commitment to an institution, thus curtailing the juvenile's freedom, the child and his parents must be advised of the child's right to counsel retained by them, or if they are unable to afford this service, counsel must be appointed to represent the child;

- right to confrontation and cross examination: the Court held that "absent a valid confession" a determination of delinquency and an order of commitment to a state institution cannot be sustained in the absence of sworn testimony subjected to the opportunity for cross examination in accordance with the law and constitutional requirement;
- privilege against self incrimination: the language of the Fifth Amendment is unequivocal and without exception and the scope of the privilege is comprehensive;
- right to transcript of the proceedings;
- right to appellate review: although the Supreme Court did not rule that a state is required by Federal Constitution to provide appellate courts and a right to appellate review, the opinion strongly recommended that appellate reviews should be available and that the transcript of proceedings at the juvenile level should include findings of fact and conclusions of law.

III. *Miranda v. Arizona*, 384 U.S. 436, 16. L. Ed. 2D 694 — The Fifth Amendment used as a basis to test the admissability of confessions. The ruling that every person, accused and being interrogated be warned:
- he has the right to remain silent;
- any statement he makes may be used as evidence against him in a court proceeding;
- he has the right to be represented by counsel, either retained or appointed, and to have him present during questioning;
- he has the right to remain silent at any time prior to or during the questioning and if he indicates he desires to remain silent during the questioning, the questioning must cease.

Glossary

Abandon	to desert, leaving a person to the mercy of someone else
Abuse	drug abuse: drugging or even poisoning, either administered directly or indirectly without prescription by medical doctor
	emotional abuse: continued inappropriate debasement of a child's feelings, rarely recognizable prior to crisis state, then manifest by externalizing — hyperactive, often anti-social acting out
	physical abuse: the perpetration of nonaccidental acts causing visible or invisible injury of variable extent to the child entrusted to care
	sexual abuse: both moral and physical insults; sexual attack usually under force and threat
Appeal	take to a higher court
Arrest	taking or keeping in custody by authority of law
Assault	to attack with force
Attorney	one who is legally appointed by another to transact any business for him, to represent him in a legal manner in a court of law
Closed hearing	not open to the public; only participants present
Commitment	to consign to a place of detention such as an institution
Concurrent jurisdiction	joint and equal in authority or jurisdiction
Curfew	designated time when juvenile must be off the streets
Custodian	one who has custody
Delinquent	any child under the age of eighteen who violates any law in the state, or any ordinance of any town, city or county in the state defining a crime or who has violated any federal law or law of another state defining a crime and whose case has been referred to the juvenile court and on the basis of facts found to be true is found to be delinquent

Delinquent act	an act committed by a young person under the age of eighteen which if he were older would be a crime under criminal statutes
Dependent	any child under the age of eighteen years of age who has no home or settled place of abode; no proper guardianship or visible means of subsistence, no parent or guardian willing to exercise or capable of exercising proper parental control; home is unfit by reason of neglect, cruelty or depravity of parent or guardian or custodian; or child who frequents the company of reputed criminals, vagrants or prostitutes or is found living in an immoral environment such as house of prostitution or assignment; who is incorrigible; is in danger of being brought up to live an idle, dissolute or immoral life; or who is habitually truant; or who uses alcohol as a beverage; who wanders about at nighttime without being on lawful business; or who is grossly and wilfully neglected as to medical care necessary for his well being
Deprivation	denial of psychological, physical or material needs to the extent that personal damage to the body or personal injury may result
Detention	to place in holding; to hold or keep as in custody
Detention hearing	hearing held to present facts to the judge which would allow him to rule whether juvenile should be held in detention pending the fact-finding and dispositional hearing, or whether he may be released pending the scheduled hearing
Diagnostic evaluation	a series of psychological, perhaps psychiatric, medical and dental tests to evaluate current emotional and physical condition of the juvenile
Dispositional hearing	a hearing concerned only with the correctional considerations of what is best for the child, or what disposition in the case seems most suited to the child's individual needs
Fact-finding hearing	the adjudicatory hearing at which time the court determines the existence or nonexistence of the allegations contained in the petition

Foster home	a home licensed by the Department of Social and Health Services to provide custody and care to children placed by order of the court or under provision of other statutes
Group home	a home licensed by the state to provide custody and care for children placed by court order or under provision of statutes usually occupied by house parents and six or more children; in some instances provides psychological and social work services
Guardian ad litem	court appointed attorney to protect the constitutional rights of the child in court hearing
Hearings	opportunity to have case of individual juvenile considered before the juvenile court judge
Incest	the crime of cohabitation between persons related within the degrees wherein marriage is prohibited by law
Incorrigible	beyond the control and power of his parents, guardian or custodian by reason of his conduct or nature
Institution	holding place for juveniles who have been adjudicated delinquent and ordered held in such a setting by the court
Juvenile court	court of jurisdiction for youths under the age of eighteen; source of referral for alleged delinquencies and dependency hearings
Juvenile court judge	presides over the juvenile court; usually a superior court judge but may be a court appointed commissioner; knowledgeable of the laws
Jurisdiction	the legal power, right or authority to hear and determine a cause or causes
Juvenile	young person usually below the age of eighteen as established by law
Legal custody	in this instance, the placement of a child in the custody of the parent, guardian or person who assumes the legal rights of parents as defined by statute
Neglect	the nonaccidental omission of basic necessities causing physical and/or emotional harm of vari-

able extent to the child entrusted for care:

educational neglect: intrinsic (system) and/or extrinsic (family) variable deficiencies

emotional neglect: lack of nurturing elements necessary to support and engender total growth

medical neglect: right of care and/or life vs. freedom of religion or parental rights

moral neglect: intangible sexual and/or criminal influences which, if uncorrected, either may corrupt, are in danger of corrupting, or have already corrupted the child

physical neglect: nonaccidental omission of basic food, shelter, clothing, and/or essential protection producing failure to thrive

Notice and Summons	legal document notifying or requiring the person having custody of the child to appear for a court hearing (the child may also receive such a document)
Official handling	involves an official hearing before the judge of the juvenile court
Open hearing	a hearing in which persons other than those immediately involved (child, parent, court staff) may sit in (this would only include those having an interest in the hearing, however, and does not invite the public in)
Petition	legal document stating the alleged charge; must be filed prior to court hearing
Probation officer	investigates the case, reports the facts to the court and supervises the probationer; officer of the court
Probation	allowing a child who has been adjudicated a delinquent to remain in the community so long as he obeys certain rules as set down by the court; may be official — imposed by the judge, or unofficial — set by the probation officer without a formal court hearing
Prosecuting attorney	attorney at law assigned to the prosecutor's office who represents the state in hearings where facts are contested
Protective supervision	supervision ordered by the court of children found to be deprived or unruly

Psychiatrist	medical doctor whose specialty is in the field of psychiatry
Psychologist	trained in the administration and interpretation of psychometric evaluation measurements; does not have a medical degree
Recidivism	a falling back into former delinquent acts; appearing before the court on an alleged delinquency following prior release after being adjudicated a delinquent
Remand	to waive jurisdictional rights in the juvenile court and refer to the prosecutor's office for determination of prosecutive merit under the adult criminal code
Resisting arrest	fighting back, an attempt to prevent an arrest from taking place
Right to counsel	under due process laws the individual has the right to retain an attorney to protect his constitutional rights and to represent him in a court of law; if he is without funds the law requires counsel be appointed for him by the court
Runaway	to leave established place of abode without permission
Shelter care	temporary care of a child in physically unrestricted facilities
Subpoena	written legal order for child and/or adult to appear in court to give testimony at the hearing
Suspended commitment	freedom to remain in the community, rather than confinement in an institutional setting so long as certain conditions of probation, as imposed by the court, are followed
Truant	absent from school without legal excuse as defined by law, such as physical illness certified by a medical doctor or emotionally unable to profit from an educational experience as certified by a medical doctor
Unofficial handling	disposition of a case made by a probation officer without benefit of a formal court hearing
Unruly	habitually truant; habitually disobedient of the lawful and reasonable commands of his parents, guardian or other custodian; ungovernable

Waiver	relinquishing a right
Ward of the court	legal custody of the child is invested in the court, and the court's order concerning the interests, welfare and well being of the child supersedes all other orders although the court may place the physical custody with the parent, guardian or custodian
Warrant	court order authorizing a law enforcement officer to make an arrest, seizure, or search or perform some other designated act
Witness	a person who because of firsthand knowledge gives evidence in court under oath

Recommended Readings

Alexander, Paul. "Constitutional Rights in the Juvenile Court," in *Justice for the Child*, M. Rosenheim, ed. New York: Free Press, 1962.

Amos, William E. "The Future of Juvenile Institutions." *Federal Probation*, March 1968, pp. 41-47.

Bender, Lauretta. "A Psychiatrist Looks at Deviancy as a Factor in Juvenile Delinquency." *Federal Probation*, June 1968, pp. 35-42.

Breckenridge, Sophanisba P., and Abbott, Edith. *The Delinquent Child and the Home*. New York: Arno Press, 1970.

Brooks, Robert. "The Highly Intelligent Delinquent." *Federal Probation*, March 1967, pp. 43-46.

Byerly, John F. "Sentencing the Juvenile Offender." *Federal Probation*, June 1962, pp. 24-26.

Coffey, Alan R. *Juvenile Justice as a System: Law Enforcement to Rehabilitation*. Englewood, NJ: Prentice-Hall, Inc., 1974.

Croxton, T. A. "The Kent Case and Its Consequence." *Journal of Family Law*, vol. 7, no. 1, 1967.

Davis, Samuel M. *The Rights of Juveniles: The Juvenile Justice System*. New York: Clark Boardman Company, Ltd., 1974.

Demsch, Berthold, and Garth, Julia. "Truancy Prevention: A First Step in Curtailing Delinquency Proneness." *Federal Probation*, December 1968, pp. 31-37.

Dobson, James. *Dare to Discipline*. Wheaton, IL: Tyndale House Publishers, 1970.

Elmer, E. "Hazards in Determining Child Abuse." *Child Welfare*, vol. XLV, no. 1, 1966, pp. 28-33.

Emerson, Robert M. *Judging Delinquents: Context and Process in the Juvenile Court*. Chicago: Aldine, 1969.

Fisher, Gary. *The Abusers*. Milford, MI: Mott Media, 1975.

Fontana, V. J. *The Maltreated Child: The Maltreatment Syndrome in Children*. Springfield, IL: Chas. C. Thomas, Publisher, 1974.

Fontana, V. J. *Somewhere a Child Is Crying*. New York: MacMillan Company, 1973.

Geis, Gilbert. "Identifying Delinquents in the Press." *Federal Probation*, December 1965, pp. 44-49.

Gibbons, Don C., and Blake, Gerald F. "Evaluating the Impact of Juvenile Diversion Programs." *Crime and Delinquency*, October 1976, pp. 411-420.

Gilman, David. "How to Retain Jurisdiction Over Status Offenses — Change Without Reform in Florida." *Crime and Delinquency*, January 1976, pp. 48-51.

Hackler, James C. "Evaluation of Delinquency Prevention Programs: Ideals and Compromises." *Federal Probation*, March 1967, pp. 22-26.

Hissong, Jerry B. "The Role of the Church in Preventing Crime and Delinquency." *Federal Probation*, December 1968, pp. 50-54.

Katz, Sanford N. *When Parents Fail: The Law's Response to Family Breakdown.* Boston: Beacon Press, 1971.

Kelley, Francis K. "The Delinquent Child: Whose Responsibility?" *Federal Probation*, December 1961, pp. 24-29.

Kempe, Henry, and Helfer, Ray. *Helping the Battered Child and His Family.* Philadelphia: J. B. Lippincott, 1972.

Kempe, Henry, and Helfer, Ray. *The Battered Child*, 2nd ed. Chicago: University Press, 1968.

King, Rufus. *The Drug Hang Up: America's Fifty Year Folly.* New York: W. W. Norton, 1972.

Lewis, Peter W., and Allen, Harry E. "Participating Miranda." *Crime and Delinquency*, January 1977, pp. 75-78.

Long, Harvey L. "The Church's Mission and Delinquents." *Federal Probation*, December 1963, pp. 26-31.

Lou, Herbert H. *Juvenile Courts in the United States.* New York: Arno Press, 1972.

Luger, Milton. *The Youthful Offender*, in the President's Commission on Law Enforcement and the Administration of Justice, Task Force Report: *Juvenile Delinquency and Youth Crime*, 1967.

MacIver, Robert M. *The Prevention and Control of Delinquency.* Chicago: Aldine, 1966.

McHardy, Louis W. "The Court, the Police and the School." *Federal Probation*, March 1968, pp. 47-52.

Martin, John N. *Juvenile Vandalism: A Study in its Nature and Prevention.* Springfield, IL: Chas. C. Thomas, 1961.

Martin, Lawrence H., and Snyder, Phyllis R. "Jurisdiction Over Status Offenders Should Not Be Removed from the Juvenile Court." *Crime and Delinquency*, October 1976, pp. 44-47.

Miller, Marshall E. "The Place of Religion in the Lives of Juvenile Offenders." *Federal Probation*, March 1965, pp. 50-53.

Neumeyer, Martin H. *Juvenile Delinquency in Modern Society*, 3rd ed. Princeton, NJ: D. Van Nostrand Company, Inc., 1961.

Paulsen, Monrad G. "The Delinquency, Neglect and Dependency Jurisdiction of the Juvenile Court," in *Justice for the Child*, M. Rosenheim, ed. New York: Free Press, 1962.

Portune, Robert. *Changing Adolescent Attitudes Toward Police.* Cincinnati: W. H. Anderson, 1971.

Protective Services for the Children of New York City: A Plan of Action. New York: Laurin Hyde Associates, 1962.

Reckless, Walter C. "A New Theory of Delinquency and Crime." *Federal Probation*, December 1961, pp. 42-51.

Robison, Sophia M. "Why Juvenile Delinquency Preventive Programs Are Ineffective." *Federal Probation*, December 1961, pp. 34-41.

Rubin, H. Ted. "The Juvenile Court's Search for Identity and Responsibility," in *Crime and Delinquency*, a Publication of the National Council on Crime and Delinquency, January 1977.

Scarpitti, Frank R., and Stephenson, Richard M. "Juvenile Court Dispositions: Factors in the Decision Making Process." *Crime and Delinquency*, April 1971, pp. 142-51.

Schepses, Erwin. "Delinquent Children and Wayward Children." *Federal Probation*, June 1968, pp. 42-46.

Thomas, Eugene S., and Sorenson, Christine. "Youth's Recipe for Success With Youth." *Federal Probation*, December 1968, pp. 26-31.

Thompson, Charles, and Poppen, William. *For Those Who Care: Ways of Relating to Youth*. Columbus: Chas. E. Merrill Publishing Company, 1972.

U.S., Federal Bureau of Investigation, Clarence M. Kelley, Director. *Crime in the United States, 1975. Uniform Crime Reports* series, August 1976.

U.S., Department of Health, Education and Welfare, Children's Bureau. *The Child Abuse Reporting Laws: A Tabular View*, 1966.

Vedder, Clyde B., and Somervill, Dora B. *The Delinquent Girl*, 2nd ed. Springfield, IL: Chas. C. Thomas, 1975.

Vinter, Robert; Newcomb, Theodore; and Kish, Rhea. *Time Out: A National Study of Juvenile Correctional Programs*. Ann Arbor: N.A.J.C., 1976.

Witherspoon, Arthur W. "Foster Home Placements for Juvenile Delinquents." *Federal Probation*, December 1966, pp. 48-52.

Young, D. J. "Is the Juvenile Court Successful?" *Federal Probation*, June 1971, p. 12.